Solo Flight

One Pilot's Aviation Odyssey around Australia

OWEN ZUPP

Copyright (c) Owen Zupp 2013

First published in 2013.

Registered Office P.O. Box 747, Bowral NSW 2576. Australia.

Author: Zupp, Owen 1964-

Title: Solo Flight. One Pilot's Aviation Adventure Around Australia.

ISBN: 978-0-9874954-1-9

Subjects: Aeroplanes. Piloting.-Biography. Air pilots, -Australia

All rights reserved. No part of this document may be reproduced, stored in a retrieval system, or transmitted in any form or by any means electronic, mechanical, photocopying, recording or otherwise without the permission of the copyright owner.

Cover Image: Over the Nation's Capital". By Paul Sadler.

Also by Owen Zupp.

'Without Precedent' - Commando, Fighter Pilot and the true story of Australia's first Purple Heart.

'The Practical Pilot' – A Common Sense Guide to Safer Flying.

'50 Tales of Flight'. From Biplanes to Boeings.

'50 More Tales of Flight'.

'Down to Earth' A Fighter Pilot's Experiences of surviving Dunkirk, the Battle of Britain, Dieppe and D-Day. (Grub Street Publishing. 2007)

www.owenzupp.com

Contents

THE AUTHOR vii

FOREWORD viii

1 SOLO FLIGHT 1

2 SOLO AROUND THE WORLD? 1

3 THERE AND BACK 8

4 GROWING WINGS 13

5 BERT HINKLER, BUNDABERG AND THE MISSING GOLD WATCH. 20

6 COMING TOGETHER 27

7 THE FINAL COUNTDOWN 36

8 D-DAY 43

9 FOUNDING FATHERS. 51

10 THE REAL OUTBACK. 59

11 DISTANT VOICES. 67

12 A HORNET'S NEST. 75

13 A BLAST FROM THE PAST. 85

14 BARE BEAUTY AND BROOME. 92

15 THE RED EARTH 102

16 A SACRED SITE. 112

17 BRIGHT LIGHTS. BIG CITY. 122

18 SOME REST AND RECREATION. 132

19 FINDING FORREST. 140

20 HEADING SOUTH. 152

21 HISTORY, HEROES AND HEARTFELT THANKS. 163

22 ACROSS BASS STRAIT. 175

23 A SPIRITUAL HOME. 188

24 HOME. 199

25 CATCHING UP. 209

26 SAFETY FIRST. 219

26 A TIME TO PAUSE. 226

28 THE FINAL APPROACH. 234

29 THE END? 242

Acknowledgements. 250

For Bert Hinkler.

***

THE AUTHOR

Owen Zupp is an award-winning writer, published author and commercial pilot with nearly 20,000 hours of flight time. He has flown all manner of machines from antique biplanes to globe-trotting Boeings and shared the journey with readers around the world in a variety of publications.

The son of a decorated fighter pilot, Owen was born into aviation. His flying career has taken him from outback Australia to the rugged mountain ranges of New Guinea, the idyllic islands of Micronesia and across the oceans of the world to the United States, Europe, Africa and beyond.

Whether witnessing rocket launches from 40,000 feet or circumnavigating Australia for charity in a tiny two-seat training aircraft, Owen has cherished every minute aloft. Flight is not merely his profession, it is his passion.

FOREWORD

I have said many times that flight is an amazing privilege.

I have been able to take many different craft into the skies at all manner of altitudes across the broadest range of speeds. And yet, sometimes the greatest pleasures in life are to be found in the simplest acts. So, it was in 2010 when I took a small two-seat aeroplane around the vast expanse of the Australian continent.

Over three weeks I hummed across some of the most diverse landscape on the planet. From deep green foliage to vast red deserts. I saw the country from above, but I was still low enough to breathe in its intimate charm. Travelling two miles each minute was ideal to absorb the majesty of the land I was witnessing and yet allowed me to traverse travel states with relative ease.

From the gun-barrel roads to the dramatic ocean cliff faces and flocks of birds that moved like massive blankets below. The people of the outback and the memorials to those who built this land were not always obvious but were well worth seeking out.

I am sure that this journey, along with the people and places will remain with me for many years to come. It was an opportunity to combine a lifelong dream and passion with a commemoration and a cause far beyond the magnitude of any individual.

I count myself truly fortunate to have undertaken this flight, and I will never again view a map of Australia in the same way. Nor will I forget that special month of May when I was able to take to the skies from Bundaberg and fly 'There and Back'.

Owen Zupp

1

SOLO FLIGHT

A nother mile and another minute passes. Uneventful and yet awe-inspiring.

Perched at altitude in my small two-seat aeroplane, the canvas below me is the vast Australian landscape. Beautifully remote, I sit in isolation with nothing but my thoughts and the task of flight to distract me from the view outside the cockpit. The instruments in front of me and the gentle hum of the controls beneath my hands assure me that all is right with the trusty little Jabiru as it cuts through air that is so very still.

It is too early in the day for the bubbles of warm air to rise and buffet me about the sky. So cool and calm, with the coastline behind me and the raw, rich reds of the inland ahead. Amidst this barren beauty, a lone patch of white seems to be wafting above the terrain like a ghostly quilt. I tilt my head and alter my focus, trying to define the sight ahead, below, and to my left. I nudge the Jabiru like a trusty horse and she moves her nose toward the alabaster carpet, gaining on it at an impressive rate.

Now closer, my eyes focus and see the faults in the stitching. For rather than a massive blanket, it is made up of many miniscule moving parts. Wings like mine but very much smaller, waving gracefully in tight formation. This is not a renegade paddock or field, but a massive flock of birds moving south. Their graceful harmony of flight makes my man-made attempt look relatively primitive, and I admire the ease with which they wheel to the left as one and continue on their way.

Geographically I am as far from home as I can be and still be flying over Australian soil. Surrounded by the country's majesty, it's hard to decide if I am halfway from my origin or halfway to my destination. I long for the familiarity of family, and yet what I have witnessed as Australia has passed by will be with me forever. There have been sights as varied as the crashing waves on rocky shores to the remote stock routes threading like capillaries across this nation. Military jet fighters have rested a wing tip away and retired giants of the sky towered over me, never to fly again. Thriving cities and isolated ghost towns, colours, sounds, sights and smells that change with every new horizon.

There is still a way to go and yet already this journey has changed me forever. This wide brown land that I call home has spoken to me in a way that can only be heard amongst the clouds and clear blue skies. And I have had to listen carefully, not distracted by the voices of others or the pressures of the day-to-day grind. To truly hear the land and understand the magic that is all around me, I have had to be alone; all alone, on this solo flight.

2

SOLO AROUND THE WORLD?

They say that a journey of a thousand miles begins with a single step. My journey began sitting down.

The credits were still running on the documentary about Ewan MacGregor's motorcycle trek when I turned to my wife and suggested that I should fly around the world solo. Yes, alone. Unstartled, her measured reply was that maybe I should start with flying around Australia. And so, the deal was struck.

This exchange with my wife occurred many months before my

wheels would leave the ground, however the genesis of such a flight was even more deeply rooted in my past. As a young charter pilot, I had driven with my father to the far side of Australia to a new job in the Kimberley township of Kununurra. Each day as we set out on that week-long drive, I was increasingly overwhelmed by the raw, expansive beauty of the land. Horizons too far away on which to focus and bounding kangaroos too close to my car for comfort.

Unloading freight in the Kimberleys

To this raw, red dirt backdrop, my Dad and I agreed to fly across Australia together one day. We had already shared a cockpit many times over the years, including those hours when he had taught me to fly. There had been many memorable moments: words of wisdom aloft, informal lunches in the shade of a wing and the odd quiet word between a father and son. Aviation had been the common thread between us from the time I was a boy when he had hoisted me up to peer into cockpits through cupped hands. It had been a common language throughout my teenage years that had meant our communication never suffered. He then mentored me until I could fly in my own right, and now it seemed like it was time for us to share the sky across Australia as peers. But that day never came.

Within a year, cancer had my father in its vile grip. The old warrior who had never walked away from a fight had finally met an enemy that he could not best. He fought each battle with the knowledge that ultimately his war was lost. He was a hero to the end, until that dark morning when his chest rose for the final time. He gasped, and then relaxed into the longest slumber.

Twenty years later, his loss seemed so far away and yet still so vivid. I now sat in my own home with the fire warming the room and my own children beside me. Part of me felt selfish for wanting to disappear for a few weeks and soar through the skies without them, but something had been stirred inside me and I knew the time for the flight had come.

It was 2009 and the following year would mark the centenary of powered flight in Australia, when the visiting American escape artist Harry Houdini had slipped the handcuffs of gravity and taken his frail flying machine into the skies. So, 2010 seemed to be an ideal time to celebrate the event by flying around Australia. The first box was ticked. However, other boxes started to emerge at a startling rate. Accommodation, fuel availability, route selection, emergency equipment, and so on. Not to mention that I might also need an aeroplane.

Dad in his fighter jet during the Korean War

As I looked at the sea of charts unfolded on my dining table, I sought to select the most appropriate route for May the following year. That month presented the best chance of favourable weather and advantageous winds. Geographically, there were certain aviation-significant places I wanted to visit, as well as landmarks from my own life and career. In the time frame available, I wouldn't be able to crawl around the entire coastal strip of this island continent and anyway, so much aviation history was connected to the remote inland. I circled towns, drew lines and measured distances.

Piece by piece, the flight began to take shape. Now I stepped back and looked at the pencil lines that circled my nation, and for the first time it struck me that this was quite a journey, even for someone with thirty years experience. I was acutely aware of safety as my first priority and considered the route in terms of terrain, water crossings and what equipment I would need to cater for all contingencies. If I couldn't execute the flight safely, then it couldn't be done at all. As they say, "Mission First. Safety Always."

Charts, flight plans and crumpled paper

My head began to spin. Would there be media coverage? Should I have a website? Should I give the flight a name? There were so many secondary issues beyond the act of flight. In fact, taking to the skies seemed like it would be the easiest aspect of the undertaking. I knew that preparation was paramount, and I had to focus on the core priorities. I set about a strategy to have everything in order from the ground up, for the success of the flight operationally would hinge upon the work in these months before departure.

With a basic route drafted, I could now grasp what was required of an aircraft to undertake the journey. My own little Piper Tomahawk was sitting in the hangar, but it didn't seem to be suited for the task. It was 30 years old and only cruised at about 95 knots, or 175 kilometres an hour. Furthermore, its endurance was such that the longest sector it could manage would only be about 4 hours before a fuel stop would be necessary. On a 7,500-nautical mile-journey, all of these operational constraints excluded the Tomahawk from being considered.

In choosing an aeroplane, firstly I assessed what I wanted the aircraft to be capable of. Ideally it would cover at least 2 miles each minute; that's a speed of 120 knots. It would be able to fly for more than 4 hours at that speed and land with reserve fuel still safely in the tanks. That would give me 500-mile legs if I needed them, which was at least 100 miles more than the Tomahawk could offer and at a higher speed.

My trusty little Piper Tomahawk (Image: 'Australian Aviation')

I would not always land at major airfields on sealed runways, so the aircraft had to be capable of outback operations. Philosophically, I also wanted the aircraft to send a positive message about aviation in Australia.

Rather than a rich man's hobby, I wanted to demonstrate the

affordability and accessibility of aviation in Australia. A business jet might make the flight a breeze, but it wouldn't send the message that I wanted folks to receive. I needed an affordable, light aircraft with suitable performance that could carry the banner for Australia's centenary of flight. But which aircraft would do that?

3

THERE AND BACK

Now I had a rough idea of the route to fly and what was required of the aircraft. What became increasingly apparent was that the project consisted of two main components: the actual flight as distinct from the maze of associated activities. As pilots are prone to do, often to the ridicule of their nearest and dearest, I made a checklist.

Execute a safe solo flight around Australia.

Select a suitable aircraft for the journey.

Define the route, considering points 1 and 2.

Support a charity.

Source an aircraft.

Establish a website.

Name the project.

Promote awareness of the upcoming flight.

The list was not definitive, but it was a start and gave me some direction.

From the outset, I knew that the flight needed to stand for more than just a pilot wending his way around Australia. I wanted to raise awareness of the work done by one particular Australian institution, the Royal Flying Doctor Service. Established in 1928, the RFDS is quintessentially Australian and had served outback communities for more than eighty years. In keeping with the Australian centenary of flight theme, the Flying Doctor seemed a logical choice, so I contacted them to gain approval to raise funds on their behalf and beneath their banner.

A Royal Flying Doctor Service 'Super King Air'

I was very clear with the Royal Flying Doctor Service that I wanted to be one step removed from the fundraising. All donations were to go directly into an online charity website, so that every dollar raised went to the RFDS. I would fund the flight out of my own pocket, and if I was lucky enough to secure sponsors, then that was great. However, under no circumstances would funds raised for the RFDS go toward my operational costs. The Flying Doctors agreed entirely, and without hesitation they approved their association with the flight. Australian cricket captain, Ricky Ponting, even signed a shirt to auction online. Another box was ticked.

Now I returned to the pressing issue of finding a suitable aircraft. I had been very fortunate to fly a variety of aeroplanes in my duties as an aviation journalist and any number of them would have undoubtedly performed admirably. In fact, the availability of a large, twin-engine, turbo-prop machine loomed, but it didn't conform to the profile that I had decided upon.

So, I drew yet another list. This time the list was of potential aircraft suppliers who I would approach about using one of their aeroplanes. I was somewhat shy and reluctant at first, although with enough media coverage this flight would undoubtedly provide a good dose of advertising for the chosen machine. Even so, I felt a little embarrassed about asking for something, for seemingly nothing.

As I hesitated in posing my request, I received a major boost in support from out of the blue. It came in the form of Robert Brus, a former Australian sailor and paratrooper with a creative entrepreneurial streak. Rob had seen service from the Middle East to Timor and was also an aviation enthusiast. He was keen to assist in any way possible, and that's exactly what he did. He set about drafting a proposal to send to aircraft suppliers while creating a brand-new website for the journey. He insisted that a web presence was needed as soon as possible, and both the website and the flight needed a name.

A few names had come to mind. Ewan Macgregor's motorcycle journey was called the Long Way 'Round, but as I was cutting inland and Ewan's copyright lawyers would undoubtedly be very proficient, I searched for another title. It came to me straight away, short and simple; 'There and Back'. Rob loved it too, so we registered the domain name and I asked the wonderful Juanita Franzi of Aero Illustrations to create a logo.

In my brief, I requested an Australian theme centred on the boomerang, which also flew there and back. I wanted the colours of both the blue Australian sky and the tones of rusty ochre to represent the outback. Juanita provided a number of options, but one stood out from the pack and it promptly became the registered trademark of the 'There and Back' around Australia flight.

The adoption of a logo and a name had a profound effect. It provided an all-encompassing identity for what had been the varied strands of a concept. Now when I spoke to aircraft suppliers, media outlets, or potential sponsors, I wasn't Owen Zupp. I was 'There and Back'. This undertaking was always destined to be far more than any individual could represent. It was a project for all to share, near and far. I was merely at the steering wheel and giving the flight a human face.

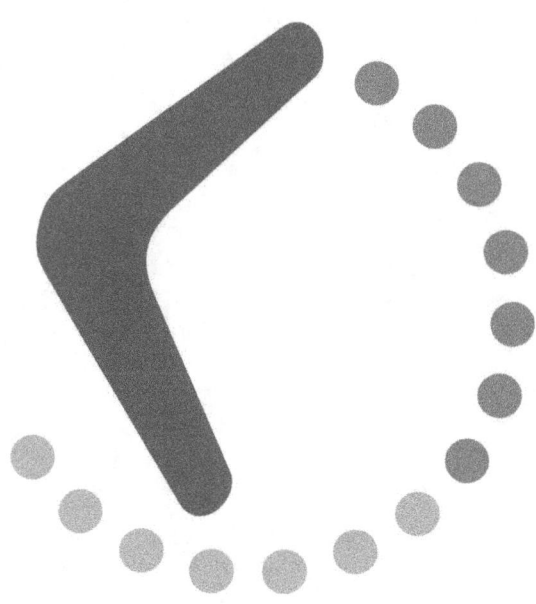

My wife, Kirrily, had been integral to the flight from the outset. She was on the phone calling motels and drawing up tabulated forms where only my hurried notes had previously existed. However, this was a substantial undertaking, and more than two of us would be needed if we were committed to getting this absolutely right.

Rob's impact was immediate, and it taught me very quickly to trust and delegate beyond the family resources. Shortly afterwards, Peter Buscall and Hayley Dean would join the team to provide flight support and media and marketing savvy respectively. 'There and Back' was now beyond the point of no return. Its momentum was too great to halt, and my magazine editors were equally excited by the concept. The low mumble began to form words and those words began to spread. Our new website was hit constantly, and the emails and phone calls started to flow in. The level of interest was overwhelming.

But just a moment...I still needed an aeroplane.

4

GROWING WINGS

Armed with a clear vision, I took a deep breath and sent off proposals to various aircraft manufacturers and distributors, humbly requesting the use of one of their aeroplanes. Some replied very quickly, others never replied at all. In the end there were three contenders, but one seemed to perfectly fit the flight's 'mission statement' of an affordable, Australian-based venture: the Bundaberg-based Jabiru.

I had visited the Jabiru factory in Queensland some months before when I wrote a story on their J230D aircraft. Capable of carrying up to four people, it would be an ideal choice for the solo flight. With only me on board, an amazing amount of equipment could be carried while still filling the tanks to their filler caps. It would cruise at my desired two miles per minute and give me a range of close to

600 miles with reserves. Furthermore, the aeroplane was Australian-designed and built and had a purchase price about the same as a four-wheel drive motor vehicle.

Sue Woods is the daughter of the Jabiru founder, Rod Stiff, and was amongst the first to reply to my request for the provision of an aeroplane for 'There and Back'. From day one, the relationship with Jabiru seemed right. Their enthusiasm and vision were identical to mine. They obviously had a passion for aviation in this wide, brown land, and together we had the opportunity to spread the message to the greater public, not merely the niche of aviation enthusiasts.

The logo of 'Jabiru Aircraft and Engines'

I could hardly contain my excitement knowing that the last major component of the foundation had been established and now the job was to build upon this. With Jabiru's commitment made public, very quickly other companies came on board; Hawker Pacific and David Clark, 'Spidertracks', Champagne PC Flight Planning, Australian Aviation and Global Aviator magazines. Through the supply of critical equipment and increasing media coverage, There and Back's pulse became a pounding heartbeat.

As Rob Brus brought the new website to life, Hayley Dean from Me Marketing began to liaise with media outlets. Radio stations, TV networks, and newspapers were all interested in the fact that this was an all-Australian affair marking an Australian centenary. However, for the moment, the general response was "Fantastic! Please contact us closer to the date." I only hoped that there would be time "closer to the date."

A Jabiru J230D off the coast of Bundaberg (Photo: Jabiru)

I now had solid performance data on a real aeroplane to work with. I sat down with my charts to one side and the new computer flight-planning software to the other. I confess to be a Luddite in some ways and carefully drew my pencil lines with their 10-mile markers across forty maps. Once I had done this in long-hand, I then entered the flight route into the computer as a second line of defence. Fortunately, everything matched.

There were so many places on my 'to-see' list. Longreach, the home of QANTAS, Tindal, Australia's northern fighter base, Darwin, where the pioneer aviators first touched down on their flights from England, my old stomping ground of Kununurra in the beautiful Kimberleys, the pioneer aviators' graves at Murchison Station, Woomera and its space heritage, Point Cook, the spiritual home of the Royal Australian Air Force, Toowoomba, my family's original hometown and my father's final resting place...the list went on and on. 8,000 nautical miles and a continent full of wonder.

I continued to draw more circles and rub out lines as either fuel availability was an issue, or there was no accommodation left in town. In the end a circumnavigation of sorts was etched out, as much defined by history as geography. Unfortunately, there were people and places that would be bypassed, including my own sister in Cairns. Nevertheless, the route that emerged filled me with anticipation as I finally stepped back from the charts and looked at the miles that I was destined to fly. I couldn't wait for the next six months to pass.

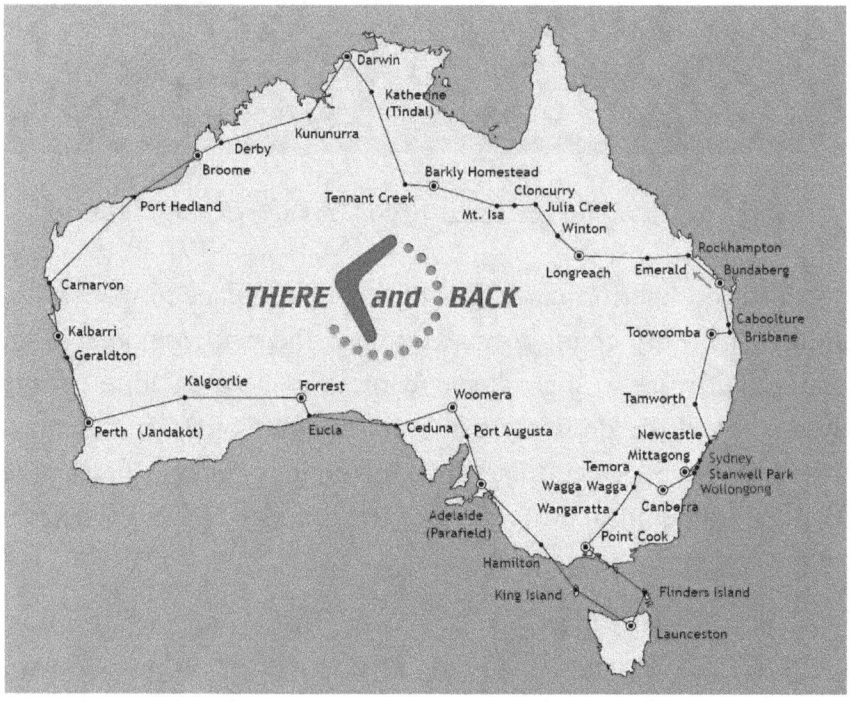

The Original Route of 'There and Back'

Of all the wonderful equipment provided by the sponsors of the flight, one particular piece took my interest. It was provided by Rob Brus in his role with a company called Spidertracks. This inconspicuous black box was not much larger than a television remote control and plugged into the aircraft's cigarette lighter outlet. Sitting on the dashboard, this aerial used satellite technology to beam my position back to a nominated web address, allowing people to track my flight on their computers.

Even better, Rob had designed a phone app for portable tracking. Every six minutes my position, ground speed and altitude would be beamed across the Internet. Additionally, in the case of an emergency, I could hit a button for more rapid updating of my whereabouts and an alert would be sent immediately to nominated phone numbers. The Spidertracks system was a great device to have on board for both safety and connecting with the public. It also reminded me that although I was flying solo, I had the Internet on the seat beside me. So don't mess up!

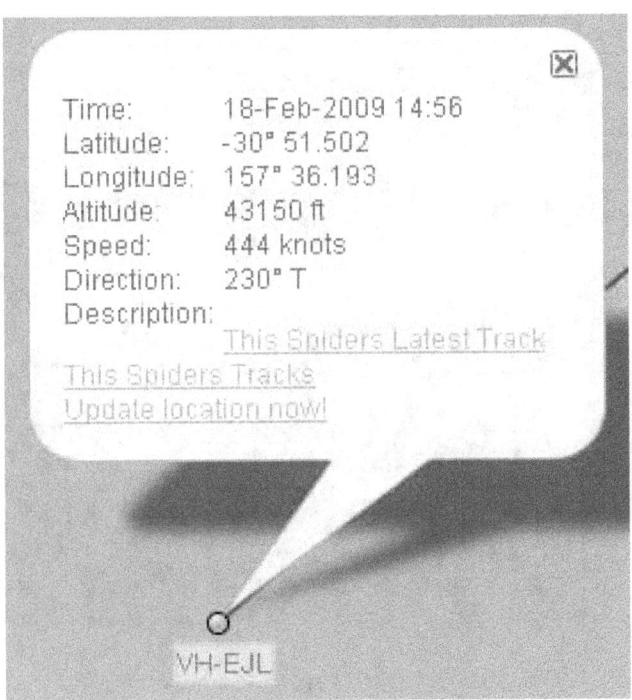

A Spidertracks display as followers would see the flight on the Internet

As I busily went about my planning and emailing, the Jabiru team had decided to build a new J230 especially for the flight. It was exciting news and the thought of flying a brand-new aeroplane around Australia gave the entire project a very shiny new edge. However, with Christmas looming, I wondered if there would be sufficient time to build an entire aircraft by the departure date in May. And not just build the aeroplane, but equip it and have it flown enough to 'bed' the engine in.

I needn't have worried as an email arrived from Sue Woods showing the aircraft laid out on the factory floor. Like a massive Airfix model, the bare white components were arranged in an orderly manner, eagerly awaiting assembly. Over the coming weeks these pieces would morph into a sleek-looking aircraft, resplendent in the markings of 'There and Back'.

The Jabiru J230D ready to take shape

For now, the aircraft, like the entire project, was a maze of components that needed to be put together in the right order. And just like the Jabiru, if it was to be completed in a timely fashion, more than one set of hands was needed. I was fortunate to have a team behind me attending to the details as I made the broad brushstrokes and focused on the flying. There was no doubt that this was a significant exercise in logistics, but the romance of the flight was never far away either. Furthermore, an unforeseen mystery and disappointment was lurking just around the corner.

5

BERT HINKLER, BUNDABERG AND THE MISSING GOLD WATCH.

Bert Hinkler (Photo: State Library of Queensland)

Sometimes luck can be in your favour and other times, not.

On this occasion, my big slice of luck stemmed from where Jabiru chose to establish their business many years before. It was the Queensland township of Bundaberg, but more than that, it was the birthplace of

Australian pioneer and solo aviator, Bert Hinkler. Their local hero was not only revered, he was commemorated in the newly-built Hinkler Hall of Aviation. Furthermore, alongside this modern facility stood Bert Hinkler's English home, Mon Repos. In 1983, it was lovingly brought to Australia and re-assembled brick by brick and nail by nail.

Hinkler's Mon Repos

Lieutenant Hinkler served with the Royal Naval Air Service (RNAS) during World War One and was also decorated. However, his fascination with flight pre-dated the conflict. As a boy, he studied birds closely and made successful glider flights on the dunes near his home. In 1928, after serving post-war as a test pilot with Avro, Hinkler finally made his flight to Australia alone, in a tiny Avro Avian, and in only 15 days. He went on to achieve several feats, but none more significant or more overlooked than his 1931 flight from Canada to South America, across the South Atlantic to Africa, and on to London in a DH Puss Moth. Always tending to avoid the spotlight, Hinkler tragically died in 1933 on a hillside in the Tuscan Mountains of Italy while undertaking yet another brave solo attempt.

He was my boyhood hero. An early knight of the skies who had crossed the globe, solo, in his frail machines with a Times Atlas on his lap to guide his way. Goggles fixed to his leather helmet with the cold slipstream sliding past his face. Mile after mile, border after border, continents came and went. In his time, there was no certainty of what lay ahead, no comforts, and certainly no GPS or Spidertracks. There was purely a compass and courage.

Between Bundaberg being Bert's home where he first soared over the sand dunes and the place where Jabiru aircraft were now built, there was no other logical place to begin and complete my solo flight. The history blended with the practicality to offer a synergy that I never could have organised. It was a good omen, if one believes in fate's hand.

My familiarisation flying was planned with Peter McNamara at ASK Flying School in Bundaberg. Consisting of some upper airwork and circuit training, the Bundaberg weather proved fickle with low clouds and showers a constant source of interruption. During the rare breaks in the weather, I managed to string together enough sessions under Peter's tutelage to feel comfortable in the J230D. Then, I flew a series of solo 'touch and go' landings to consolidate my feel for the aeroplane.

The Hinkler Hall of Aviation in Bundaberg

Here comes the weather again. Let's head for home.

As I sat on the river bank one afternoon following a session of takeoffs and landings, I pondered how far aviation had come since Bert Hinkler crossed the globe. Part of me wished that he could step through time and climb on board with me to witness how much of his aviation vision became reality. To hand him control of a composite-built aeroplane with an enclosed cockpit, heater, and coloured TV screens for instruments where he had only known rudimentary dials.

Unfortunately, I did not have a means of tearing the fabric of time and transporting Bert into this day and age. However, I thought he may well be able to make the journey with me in a slightly less physical form. To this end, I set about scanning the Internet and auctions for a possession of Bert's that could circumnavigate Australia with me. At the end of the flight, this item would find a new home at the Hinkler Hall of Aviation. The concept seemed sound; now I just needed the memento.

I wasn't sure what that item would be as I scrolled through the online auction catalogues, and then something hit me out of the blue. An auction in England appeared online for a gold watch presented to Bert Hinkler in 1928, following his solo flight from England to Australia. This was perfect!

I knew that the watch wouldn't come cheap, but it seemed the perfect piece for my journey and, ultimately, to call Bundaberg home. I researched the engraving on the casing and found an old newspaper reference to Bert speaking with the group that presented him with this pocket watch. Through every resource that I could muster, this watch seemed like the real deal, so I scraped together my pennies and waited to bid.

The night of the auction, I paced the floor beside my computer as the minutes counted down. As the second hand zeroed in, my finger hovered over the mouse; it was all or nothing. And then, click. It was done. Within seconds, the colour of the font on the screen in front of me confirmed that I had won the auction. I now owned Bert Hinkler's pocket watch, and it was coming home to Bundaberg! I was over the moon...for about eight hours.

Bert Hinkler's Pocket Watch

When I awoke the next morning, my inbox was full of e-mails relating to my newly-acquired memorabilia. However, far from congratulatory, they contained disturbing content from an under-bidder and the vendor. I had inadvertently walked into a situation that involved everyone, from Interpol to the South African police. Astounded and a little panicked, I tried and decipher the conversations for the real story. I had already transferred the significant funds and was now wondering what drama in which I had become entwined.

Slowly, an unfortunate story emerged. The under-bidder was a knowledgeable individual who had previously traced the origins of the watch and sought to give the watch a proper home. His search revealed that the watch had been stolen from the home of Bert Hinkler's stepdaughter in South Africa years before. He was now seeking to return it to its rightful owner, and he had been in contact with Interpol about the stolen watch.

I sided with the under-bidder that we should recover the watch one way or the other. E-mails and phone calls began to fly between the vendor, myself, and the under-bidder, as well as the Hinkler Hall of Aviation. Then, without warning, the auction was retracted, my monies refunded, and the watch disappeared from the face of the earth. The vendor no longer replied to any of my e-mails and the path went very cold, very quickly. Bert Hinkler's wonderful gold watch had gone underground.

My disappointment was obvious, as I thought there had been a real opportunity to preserve a slice of history. On a more positive note, the under-bidder and I continued to correspond after the event as he was also a long-term admirer of Bert Hinkler. So much so, that one day a letter arrived from his address in Victoria. Inside, carefully packaged, was Bert Hinkler's autograph on an old piece of paper. I may not have a gold watch to carry with me, but I now had a tangible link to Bert. It was time to re-focus on the flight as the weeks continued to tick down toward departure.

6
COMING TOGETHER

The departure date of May 5th had once seemed an epoch away. Now it was closing in with the speed of a missile and I was squarely in its path. And as the date grew closer, so did the media interest and the requests for interviews. Kirrily compiled a growing list of confirmed accommodation and contact details, as I communicated with the various bodies I was to deal with and the growing list of folks I would address along the way.

In the midst of the preparations, my wife and I stole away for a few days of relative rest and recreation. However, rather than an island escape, we travelled to Victoria, where the centenary of Harry Houdini's first powered flight in Australia was being celebrated. At a place called Digger's Rest in 1910, Houdini had taken his frail

Voisin biplane into the skies and astutely had the event recorded and photographed, thus installing his effort as the first documented powered flight in Australia.

Now in March, a century later, Kirrily and I drove toward the air show being held in honour of the event. Our arrival was greeted in the first instance by a little Cessna making a very low approach to the airfield at Melton and all but having a collision with the tour bus ahead of us! Having survived the near roadside mid-air collision, we spent the day wandering about the aircraft on display while others roared and soared overhead. Our friend, Guy Bourke, even made a flying visit in a P-40 Kittyhawk.

Guy Bourke makes a pass in the Kittyhawk

But for all the fanfare, my thoughts were elsewhere. There was a plot of land far from the madding crowd that I needed to visit. It was the actual pasture where Houdini's flight had taken place and despite the power of the internet and Google Maps, it was not easy to find. After a series of false directions, wrong turns, and the day growing older, we finally located a small inconspicuous stone cairn by the roadside with a plaque on top. This was it.

We brought the car to a halt and stepped onto the verge. The little monument sat alone and uncared for with rotting boxes and an empty bottle of Jack Daniels lying against its side. The plaque explained what took place nearby one hundred years before and directed my gaze to look up and toward a thicket of trees a few hundred yards away. For it was just beyond these trees that Houdini leapt into our history books.

A forgotten landmark of Australia's first powered flight

I was caught with mixed emotions. I was in awe that I was only metres away from the site of a major piece of Australian history and that the patch of air just over the way was where it all began. And then I was torn by this small, forgotten, neglected memorial. Even in the centenary year, no one had bothered to clean around this plinth in its serene little setting. We contemplated the scene for quite some time before the wind picked up. A wind far too strong for the Voisin to ever cope with, I suspect.

We moved back to the car and went on our way. I was now even more determined to remind people of Australia's proud aviation heritage and how this island continent had fought well above its weight in this field of endeavour. This sad little marker on the side of the road deserved better, as did the memories of all those who have gone before in the pursuit of the skies. If not inspired, my resolve was definitely reinforced.

Meanwhile, inspiration was not in short supply in Bundaberg. While we were contemplating the events at Digger's Rest, the Jabiru factory continued with astounding speed their task of building the There and Back Jabiru 230D. At each stage of construction, Sue sent me a photograph of the aircraft and put together they would have made an amazing piece of time-lapse photography. In twenty days, the Airfix kit had grown into an aircraft waiting to take to the skies.

The Jabiru J230D grew from this...

...to this...

...in just twenty days!

The next stage of the aeroplane's development was the test flying schedule. Again, the weather prevented the Jabiru from escaping the confines of the factory and Mother Earth, except for a brief engine run. Having experienced weather delays during my own Jabiru training, I wondered if this was to become the Achilles heel for my solo flight. Finally, the weather cleared, and Jamie Cook started to see just how well the aircraft had come together, and, by all indications, it was a winner.

Now that the Jabiru assumed its full form, it also gained an identity. It was now entered on the Recreational Aviation Australia registry as 24-7381, or as I was to transmit many times over the radio, "Jabiru-73-81". From the photographs it looked fantastic, and I couldn't wait to see 73-81 up close. As it turned out, I wouldn't have to wait long. In the meantime, I pencilled a scheme for the aircraft, and the Jabiru factory set about creating the required decals in-house, although the unveiling would have to wait until much closer to the day.

My first draft of the Jabiru's There and Back scheme

Seeing the aeroplane for the first time at a gathering at Temora Airport was a thrill. It was a very tangible link to the journey that I was preparing to embark upon. As it sat in the Jabiru chalet at Temora, I paused at a distance and surveyed the J230's lines and pinched myself that this was the very aircraft in which I would circumnavigate Australia. This composite form with its wings, engine, and instruments was to become my constant companion and most trusted friend for three weeks, yet we were still effectively strangers.

I wandered closer and viewed 73-81 from different perspectives as interested buyers lined up to sit inside her and feel the controls beneath their hands. I, too, was keen to slide into the pilot's seat, but I had to wait my turn. Patiently, I wandered over and chatted to Sue Woods, whom I had taken by surprise. She quickly informed me how well the Jabiru performed on the flight down from Bundaberg, fuel-efficient and fast. It was a well-built machine.

The 'There and Back' Jabiru 230D before donning her new scheme

In a brief pause between potential customers, Jamie Cook confirmed everything Sue had said and encouraged me to take a seat inside. I slipped into the left seat and felt at home straight away. Knowing what lay ahead, they kindly doubled-up on the seat cushioning and my backside appreciated the forethought immediately. My eyes skipped around the cockpit at all the toys that lived therein. Dynon digital multi-function displays, Garmin GPS, standby instruments, digital transponder, and so on. My mind also drifted back to Bert Hinkler and the Spartan open cockpit of his Avro Avian. We had come a long way in a relatively short time.

My first look inside 73-81

With throttle in my left hand and my right on the yoke, I could almost see the miles ahead. There was no sense of trepidation in the slightest, only impatient anticipation. I knew that the preparation had been thorough; I had good equipment, good support, and a good team. If the weather played the game, there was no reason why I couldn't execute this flight just as it was planned. Sitting in the cockpit gave me an added sense of confidence, but not a single ounce of complacency. The job was still to be done.

The aircraft's metamorphosis from a series of disconnected pieces in many ways paralleled the progress of the project. What had started as an idea consisting of varied strands had come so far to become a consolidated unit. Each component relied upon the others to work in unison for the entire project to function successfully. With the help of a wonderful wife, a great team, and supportive sponsors, we reached that point.

Everyone did all that they could to ensure that we were ready when May 2010 arrived. Now it was here; it was up to me to do 'that flying thing' and not put all their good work to waste. This wasn't a burden; it was a reminder that this flight was to be flown by me, but about everything else. It was about raising funds for the RFDS. It was about making people aware of our aviation heritage and that all children can still dream of the wonder of flight. It was about the beauty of endless miles over an incredible country. It was about Bert Hinkler. It was about a small neglected plaque on a Victorian roadside. There was a major aviation gathering to take place in New South Wales over Easter, and the plan was to fly the Jabiru down for the event. It would not only serve to showcase the Jabiru, but also provide a wonderful proving-flight for both the airframe and engine. It was a three-hour drive from my home, but a significantly longer flight from Bundaberg to Temora, NSW.

7

THE FINAL COUNTDOWN

So, it all came down to this. A few carefully-packed kit bags on the floor of my study and one more sleep left in my own bed. The last six months had been so intense from a planning perspective that I now simply wanted to go flying. I wanted to replace preparation and speculation with outback airstrips and golden coastlines.

My journey north to the starting line began as a passenger in a QANTAS Boeing 767 to Brisbane. As the early morning fog was replaced by drizzling rain, I waited to board the flight at a gloomy

Sydney Airport. My four children buzzed around with excitement and a tinge of sadness that echoed my own emotions. I reassured them that I'd see them again in a couple of weeks on my way around, and I promised Ruby that I would be back for her birthday. Meanwhile, my baby boy stared through the glass windows at the row of parked airliners, teetering there and threatening to take his first steps. Would that happen while I was away?

I reassured my kids with the fact that I was away for more time and at a greater distance in the days when I flew internationally, but that seemed a cold consolation as the announcement was made to board the aircraft. I kissed the little ones and my gorgeous wife, and slung my camera gear over my shoulder, and headed down the aerobridge. From my seat, I could still see little Hayden leaning against the glass as the Boeing pushed away from the terminal and started its engines. Minutes later, I was on my way and the only view outside was that of more aeroplanes, taxiways, and the persistent rain.

During the flight, I intentionally switched off for an hour and endeavoured to rest my mind amidst a sea of spinning thoughts. I was partially successful, but my slumber was broken by the familiar sound of the wheels being lowered into the airflow on the approach to land. I was traveling with minimal baggage, having ferried equipment to Queensland over the previous weeks, and Kirrily's parents had assembled a range of emergency gear and rations at my destination. The balance of my supplies was already loaded in their car when they met me at Brisbane Airport for the drive to Bundaberg.

My kids wave goodbye at Sydney Airport

The drive was relaxing with the conversation complementing mile after mile. Outside, the rain continued to fall in dribs and drabs, and I flicked up the latest weather chart on my phone. A high-pressure system was threatening to push this coastal weather out to sea and my fingers were crossed that it would. That would mean fantastic weather for my departure and the first few days at least, but if the 'High' failed to gain the upper hand, it could see me grounded at Bundaberg.

Sure enough, my arrival at Bundaberg was greeted with sporadic rain showers as I moved my gear into my hotel room. I laid everything out on the benches, charged up my array of electronic devices, and bid a grateful farewell to Kirrily's parents. After a room service meal, I completed my diary for the day, answered emails, and called it an early night for I knew that the next few days were destined to be very busy. And so they were.

The morning dawned with clear skies, although the gloomy weather system still loitered off the coast. I took a taxi to the airfield early the next day and on arrival, Jabiru Aircraft promptly supplied me with a car. The greeting from Sue Woods and the staff was one of excited, enthusiastic warmth. I felt right at home with these good people and knew that my choice of aeroplane had been correct on so many levels. Without delay, I was taken to see the J230D, which was parked outside the hangar, waiting for me to take her flying.

There she sat. Adorned in her 'There and Back' markings, the Jabiru looked immaculate. From the boomerang logo to the RFDS crest and route map on her flanks, the aeroplane looked ready to set course for the far side of the great southern land, there and then. I couldn't wait to set off, but for the moment the two of us needed to get to know each other better.

The morning was interspersed with media commitments ranging from television's Channel Ten to the Bundaberg News Mail newspaper. Having answered a series of questions about the aircraft, the flight, and the cause, I was able to at last take to the skies in 73-81.

Jabiru 73-81 in all her 'There and Back' finery

Before I started the engine, I carefully scanned my checklists and every switch and control. All was in order and now the sky beckoned as the wooden propeller flicked over and the engine burst into life.

It was just me, the Jabiru, and the camera gear sitting behind my right shoulder as we rolled along the taxiway and out to the runway's end. I ran the engine up to near full power, and she purred as I checked the temperatures, pressures, magnetos, and all manner of items. I briefed myself on the emergency procedures and critical airspeeds for the takeoff, but now there was nothing left to do...except fly.

That first takeoff was magical. The Jabiru tracked along the centreline under the gentle squeeze of my rudder pedals, as she accelerated with just a subtle kick in my pants. As the runway lights whizzed by in my peripheral vision, I eased back on the control column, and for the first time, 73-81 and I were airborne together. It was a wonderful sense of freedom as I wheeled the Jabiru onto the downwind leg for a series of takeoffs and landings with Bundaberg township sitting just outside my window. There were checks to complete and attention to be paid, but this flight was an absolute pleasure and captured on the digital video camera that sat beside me. However, ominous clouds were brewing on the horizon.

All too soon the flight was over, but I taxied back with absolutely nothing to report and nothing needing adjustment. The aeroplane was ready to go, and my subsequent short flights in the next 24 hours were purely for my familiarisation and for an airborne reprieve from the non-stop phone calls. Many of those calls came from the media as Hayley Dean did her best to coordinate interviews between my flights and other tasks. She did an incredible job as the interest seemed to be growing exponentially while the countdown to departure grew closer. The ABC, Courier Mail, Channel Ten, and radio stations from Mount Isa to Launceston were all fascinated by the flight ahead. Their interest was also converting into donations for the Royal Flying Doctor Service as I watched the total rise on the dedicated fund-raising website.

Practise makes perfect. I run through a wheel change on the Jabiru.

The day prior to departure now dawned wet and grey. Those clouds had rolled back in overnight, and the dripping outside my hotel room was persistent from about 3 a.m. Back at the airfield, I ran through a number of fundamental maintenance procedures with Jamie Cook and the engineers at Jabiru Aircraft. From wheel changes to battery replacement, oil and filter changes, and the removal of the cowling for the daily inspection I would perform each morning. It was educational and reassuring to run through these tasks one by one, even though I hoped there would be no need to perform them in anger. They increased my level of knowledge and confidence in the aeroplane. I felt that I had prepared for as many contingencies mechanical, meteorological, and otherwise over the preceding months, so now I just had to concentrate on flying.

After few more interviews and a few more phone calls, I loaded the aeroplane with my gear and a series of spare parts, jumper leads, emergency rations, water and remote area survival equipment. Flight plans were completed and there was nothing to do but go back to my hotel room and sleep.

The rain continued to fall, but I was confident that the high-pressure system and fine weather would ultimately win out. As I lay down that night, the excitement level was at its peak and yet I was still able to sleep soundly. The combination of my mental checklist being completed, and the drum of the rain gave me an inner peace. My breathing grew slower, and my eyes were heavy. Sleep came easily, as easily as the rain running down the roof above.

8
D-Day.

Dawn at Bundaberg.

Day One. Bundaberg to Emerald.

D-Day. Departure Day. It is 5 a.m. and all is quiet outside.

I hurry and look out the window of my hotel room to see that the high-pressure system has won the battle overnight. The sky is absolutely crystal clear and illuminated by the first rays of dawn in one direction and the waning of the twinkling stars in the other. I could not have hoped for a better sight, and I hurriedly log onto my computer to check the latest weather forecasts and charts. The news is all good, in fact, it is perfect. Not only is the weather to the west look clear, but the winds on the back curve of the 'high' should give me a favourable little push through the skies.

Without delay, I fax my flight plan details to Peter Buscall back in Sydney where he will maintain a Search and Rescue watch as he follows my flight. I shower, shave, and pack my gear, then make my way to the dining room at the Villa Mirasol for a full breakfast to the most perfect of settings. The flight is a 'go', and in a few hours I will begin my journey around Australia. You beauty!

At Bundaberg Airport there is an air of excitement. As preparations for the arrival of dignitaries are attended to at the passenger terminal, I complete the loading of the aircraft outside of the hangar. Even with the mass of equipment I have on board, the load does not even reach the bottom sills of the windows and the aircraft remains well below its maximum takeoff weight. All that remains is to refuel '73-81' and get on my way.

It is an hour prior to my planned 10 a.m. departure as I taxi the Jabiru to the bowser on the main tarmac. As I round the corner I can see the small crowd gathering, intermingled with the cameras, cables and boom microphones of the media. Inside I feel a subtle mixture of excitement and anticipation, but overwhelmingly my mind is on the job at hand. The first day, the first sector, the first takeoff.

Fortunately, the fuel bowser is a distance away from the centre of excitement, allowing me to refuel in an unhurried manner and arrange my cockpit and charts, so that I will be able to climb aboard and depart speedily when the time comes. For the moment, though, I shake hands and warmly thank the people for the tremendous support they have shown me. Local councillors, newspapers, TV channels, radio stations, and representatives from the Hinkler Hall of Aviation are all here, as well as the good folks of Bundaberg. I am humbled by the turnout and take care not to rush the moment, as keen as I am to start flying.

A last wave farewell

The Mayor hands me a parcel of 'letters of welcome' from Bundaberg to hand to the Mayors of other Australian townships along the way. It is a significant gesture and reminds me of the far reach of this flight. The act also serves to nicely round off formalities and cue me to wave farewell as I climb aboard the Jabiru.

Aware that everyone is waiting for that 'last goodbye' moment, I start 73-81 and taxied her away from the tarmac area to the engine run-up bay. Here, I thoroughly check that everything is in order and brief myself for the departure to Emerald one last time. The load behind me is lashed down, and I am strapped in. I feel in my pocket for Bert Hinkler's autograph. It is safe and secure.

On my way around Australia

The breeze is light, and the sky is beautifully blue as I line the Jabiru up on Bundaberg's Runway 14. I smoothly ease the throttle forward, and the engine smoothly responds. The wheels begin to turn with increasing pace as the acceleration forces me back into my seat, and the blades of grass outside begin to blend into a blur of green. The engine instruments tell me that all is in order, and the airspeed indicator tells me that it is time to fly. 73-81 is already starting to raise her nose as I gently pull back on the control column in my right hand. The vibration and the noise of the ground's finite runway succumb to the speed and smoothness of the limitless sky. I am on my way.

Out to my left I can see the small crowd still there waving farewell, while ahead, the coastline appears beyond the nose. I reach down and select the flaps to 'up', prompting the little electric motor to set about whirring to its task. Flaps up, after-takeoff checks complete, and a sweeping left hand turn to set course along the coast to Gladstone. I log the time on my flight plan: 4 minutes past 10 o'clock. It's an on-time departure and only a short day of flying ahead of me.

Bert fills in as the cameraman.

I level off at 2,500 feet and set the engine RPMs to 2850. From the instrumentation, I ascertain that the Jabiru is drinking fuel at the miserly rate of only 25 litres per hour and passing through the air at a brisk 117 knots. Everything is off to a copybook beginning as I fill out my flight log, check the GPS, and ensure that everything is in order. I take a deep breath and a few photographs, including one of 'Bert' on the dashboard. Bert is a small soft toy in the form of a little brown dog that my children have asked me to carry. Bert sits there in the sun, smiling, and ready for the long haul ahead. Then it hits me...

The planning and preparation was now over, and this long flight has actually begun. In my head, James Taylor's line of "10 miles behind me and 10,000 more to go" bounces around with added significance. As I turn inland, the coastal strip gives way to the greens and browns of central Queensland. Rocky ranges jut up from the undulating foliage, while ahead the visibility is unlimited, and the horizon merges earth and sky in a subtle union beyond the eye's focus. It is only the first hour and I am already captivated by the beauty of Australia's raw enormity.

I had only planned a relatively small day of flying, anticipating delays out of Bundaberg that never eventuated. The media was on time, the weather played the game, and the dignitaries were waiting for me. Consequently, it was now only a couple of hours flying to Emerald to refuel and another couple onto Longreach, where I would stay the night.

Setting course. 7,500 miles to go.

Gradually, the ranges and their eucalypts give way to the inland and mile upon mile of straw-coloured paddocks. A lone fire to the south billows grey smoke into the air, but otherwise the sky is featureless, and the land is only divided by the occasional fence or road. In the distance, a township begins to grow from the horizon. Not a metropolis, but far more than the occasional homestead and coal mine I have sighted so far. As I draw closer, the irrigated pastures showcase various shades of green, interspersed with the red soil of ploughed fields. In their midst sits the long black strip of asphalt that is Emerald Airport.

As I position to land, the only other chatter on the radio is a lone King Air, a Flying Doctor inbound to Emerald. How appropriate I muse, that the first aircraft I hear is one of the very aircraft that I am flying to support. Those green pastures grow closer as does the black tar, and before long the Jabiru's wheels are once again reunited with the planet and on their way to the fuel bowser.

First stop: Emerald, Queensland.

As I climb up to refuel the Jabiru's wings, I chat with a young charter pilot who is whittling away the hours while his passengers are in town conducting their business. We share a joke and a little bit of pilot brotherhood as the cool AVGAS pours into the tanks. I couldn't help but reflect how many hours I had spent wandering around airports, stretched out on terminal benches, or peering through the cracks in hangar doors. It is part of a pilot's journey, and for me it was decades ago, but still, in some ways, it was only a heartbeat away.

Refreshed and re-supplied, I start the Jabiru and ready myself for another takeoff. However, another Flying Doctor is on the move. I park the brakes and sit back, letting the RFDS aircraft go by and depart first as, undoubtedly, his commitments are more pressing than mine. As he taxied past my little Jabiru, he must have caught a glimpse of the RFDS crest on the nose of my aeroplane as he transmitted a little "Good Luck!" over the radio and gave me a thumbs up. The brotherhood is alive and well.

As the King Air rapidly disappears from sight, I enter the runway and track back to the white stripes at the threshold before turning around to depart. All clear, I release the brakes and open the throttle, sending 73-81 rolling down the pavement. Lifting off, we are on our way again. Another short hop, but this one will take me to the home of one of Australian aviation's founding fathers.

9

FOUNDING FATHERS.

The original QANTAS hangar

Day One. Emerald to Longreach.

Nine decades in two hours, give or take. That is the equation.

No, I haven't found the elusive answer to 'warp speed', however I am now setting course for the origins of Australia's national carrier ninety years earlier. The destination is the outback city of Longreach, and the airline is the Queensland And Northern Territory Aerial Services, or QANTAS.

Emerald falls away behind me as the Jabiru and I set course to the northwest over yet more expansive plains. There is a green tinge to the earth below which provides sound evidence of the rains that have fallen in recent months, after years of drought. Even now, a few towering Cumulus clouds water random paddocks, and I nudge to the left and right to remain clear of these downpours. Little havens like Alpha and Jericho pass by beneath the nose of the aircraft as the miles to Longreach and the first day's flying counts down.

The Jabiru hums along as I tick off waypoints on my chart and flight plan. It is only the first day, but already I am making better time and using less fuel than I had planned. Preparing for the worst and being pleasantly surprised is always a sound philosophy in aviation. Glancing at my panel-mounted GPS and its multi-coloured wealth of information, I can't help but think of the pioneer aviators. They were exposed to the elements and so often unsure from where their next supply of food or fuel was coming.

Even below me, the roads are a far cry from the muddy tracks that the pioneers traversed. It was along these muddy lines in the scrub that two of the founders of QANTAS had driven a Model T-Ford in 1919 to survey the route for an air race. At the end of the arduous 51-day journey, Hudson Fysh and Paul McGinness were left with no doubt of the aeroplane's future in such territory. The two veterans of World War One then combined with another veteran and wealthy grazier Fergus McMaster to found QANTAS in 1920. Along with the engineering expertise of Arthur Baird, the foundations were laid for one of the world's greatest airlines.

The QANTAS Model-T Ford (Photo: State Library of Queensland)

Their first aircraft had been an open-cockpit biplane from World War One, an Avro 504K. Now, my Jabiru is scooting through the skies at nearly twice the speed of a '504' and weighing 200kg less than the Avro. Furthermore, the trusty little J230D can fly three times as far as the biplane in a heated cabin with every radio, instrument, bell, and whistle you could desire. My luxury further emphasises the enormity of the challenges they faced in those pioneering times.

Back in the present, Barcaldine passes by right on time, and I have another thirty minutes until I arrive at Longreach. I run through my checks and ready my cockpit for the end of the first day. Reaching back, I adjust the camera to film the landing out of the passenger's side window to change the angles from time to time. Now I just have to remember to turn it on.

Longreach Ahead

Roads converge from the left and right, and then Longreach looms through the spinning disc of the Jabiru's propeller. I pitch the aircraft slightly nose-down and begin the descent to the airport which sits a few miles from the town. Even at a distance, it is obvious that this is not your typical country airport as the gigantic form of a Boeing 747 sits to one side, surrounded by other airframes that are twinkling in the afternoon sun.

As I sweep overhead, I see that the 747 is flanked by a DC-3 and a Boeing 707. Three of the all-time great aircraft of civil aviation have gathered together once more in a space about the size of a football field. I shelve the pleasant distraction until I land and focus on flying the aeroplane. I appear to be the only aircraft in the area as I line up for my final approach, now with the flaps fully extended and the camera running to capture any embarrassing moments. As if to appease the camera, the Jabiru sits smoothly 'in the slot' as the grass-edged asphalt grows ever closer. I ease the throttle and the yoke back, and the aircraft responds gently. Her nose a little higher and the engine a little quieter, and then the wheels make contact.

The Longreach Fleet (Photo: QANTAS Founders Museum)

I roll out to the far end of the runway and taxi to the apron where a Dash-8 airliner is parked, awaiting its passengers. I transmit my arrival to 'Brisbane Radio' and reverently pass the giant QANTAS airliners of yesteryear who form the most impressive welcoming committee I could ask for. Bringing the aircraft to a halt, I park the brakes, confirm all my engine indications are normal, check the magnetos, and then shut the engine down. The Jabiru's propeller comes to a halt, and my first sector of flying solo around Australia is over, but the day is still far from done. Across the way sits the QANTAS Founders Museum, and while time is short, I must at least make a flying pass through its hallowed halls.

The QANTAS Founders Museum

The sun is getting lower as I refuel and tie down the Jabiru in what is to become a daily ritual. Safe and secure, I remove my 'nav bag', overnight gear, camera equipment, laptop computer, GPS, and headsets. All up the weight of the large black kitbag is substantial as I sling it over my shoulder and lift my 'nav bag' in my free hand. At this moment, I am thankful that all my accommodation has generally provided transport or is within a reasonable walking distance from the airfield.

I enter the QANTAS Founders Museum to find mementos from every era of the QANTAS story. The history of those first pioneers is outlined, recounting their war service in Palestine and how the great airline ever came to be. Posters and plates from another bygone era relate to when air travel was more akin to a cruise-liner with extended layovers in exotic ports of call. Uniforms, engines, film, and photographs; it is all here. And that's not forgetting the fleet of aeroplanes now at rest outside.

It seems incongruous that such a modern museum is located relatively remotely, but then again, it makes perfect sense. For these are the lands that QANTAS first sought to cross, and these are the communities that they first sought to serve. While the very first home base was Winton, it was only a matter of months before Longreach became the thriving headquarters for the fledgling airline and even the site where they built their own aeroplanes. Yes, Longreach oozes the history of QANTAS and to locate it in some urban hub may place it near the populous, but would it really capture the airline's spirit?

After a little more pondering, I hitch a ride with the owner of the Jumbuck Motor Inn where I am to spend the night. I am more than a little exhausted by the time I make it to my room and unpack to sit down and write my blog for the newspaper, website, and all of the media following the flight. I type away and download images before sending off the long line of e-mails and phone calls from radio stations. My head is spinning as I write the dot points of the day in my diary and ready my gear for the next day. There is one last review of tomorrow's flight plan and the weather forecast; it looks good. All done!

I soak under the shower for quite a while, staring at the frog doing laps of the toilet bowl. My brain is numb as music from across the way at the Jumbuck's bar pumps out tune after tune into my subconscious. I darken the room and lie down, thankful for such a clockwork departure and first day, but equally thankful for the chance to sleep. My mind bounces between reflecting upon what has been and conjuring what is to come. I do my utmost to hose down the synapses that are at war in my head as the alarm clock will be buzzing all too soon.

Finally, I begin to settle. The music outside has almost reduced to a hypnotic bass beat, drumming me to sleep as my breathing slows to the rhythm. And then the beat changes, half-stirring me from my slumber as it is a song I knew from many, many years before. As a mere boy, the 7-inch black disc with its blue and white paper centre would spin on our record player at 45 rpm. I can hear it now and see my family at our little fibro home in Guildford. The words recount the exploits of 'Snoopy' and the 'Bloody Red Baron of Germany' to a boisterous tune. I think of my Dad's boisterous version of his personal favourite 40 years before, and a smile once again creeps over my face.

Snoopy Versus The Red Baron

It is four decades since I have heard Dad's song, and here I am on the flight we promised to complete together. Perhaps he has decided to make this journey with me after all. In my mind I can see him standing there, my smile widens, and I fall to sleep.

10

THE REAL OUTBACK.

Day Two. Longreach - Mount Isa - Barkly Homestead.

The alarm clock buzzes right on time as one expects, but secretly hopes otherwise.

I throw my legs over the side of the bed, start the laptop and 'flick' on the kettle. Everything from the cup of tea to my clothes are in order from the night before; ready and set to go. The weather still looks faultless along my route, so I send through the flight details over the wonder of the Internet and begin to get my gear together. I have organised an early breakfast and a lift to the airport with the good folks at the Jumbuck and I'm on my way before I know it. The sun is only just breaking the horizon, although it seems to rise more quickly in this part of the world.

Despite the early hour, I call my sister Pamela and recount the incredible coincidence of Dad's 'Red Baron' song being played the night before. We agree that neither of us have heard it since about 1969 and recall Dad's out-of-tune gusto in singing the song and his emphasis on the word "bloody". She wishes me luck and I hang up with a smile on my face, ready for the day ahead.

The Dash-8 is still parked on the tarmac from the night before as I pre-flight the Jabiru. I had fuelled the aircraft the night before, but a thorough going-over is still needed at the beginning of each day's flying. I remove the engine cowling and what lies beneath is as clean as a whistle. The engineers have fitted a small bottle to catch any oil that vents overboard to both keep the aircraft clean and monitor my oil usage. That container is empty, and the oil quantity dip-stick confirms the fact that the Jabiru hasn't used a drop on the first day. A reassuring thought as I am about to set course over the remote reaches of western Queensland and the Northern Territory.

I farewell Longreach and the Bloody Red Baron to an escort of birds emerging from the grass just as I lift off and set course to the northwest. Mount Isa, my first port of call, is about three hours away, but a great deal of history lies between here and there. This region was the early stomping grounds of both QANTAS and the Royal Flying Doctor Service, and I will be retracing many of the air routes of those early days as the Jabiru skips along its way.

Preflight Inspection

The aircraft cruises along smoothly and I cannot help but smile to the point of singing. There is not a single cloud in the sky or a ripple of turbulence. My calculations have me benefiting from a tailwind and destined to be ahead of schedule. It is absolute perfection in the context of light aircraft 'visual' flight. As a consequence, I am relaxed and enjoying every minute and mile as they pass. I stretch over, grab a Muesli Bar and enjoy some fine dining in the skies. This is living!

My first turning point is Winton. I was once told that QANTAS was conceived in Cloncurry, born in Winton, but grew up in Longreach. If that was the case, the airline's maternity ward now lies dead ahead. I had visited there once before when my Dad and I had driven to Kununurra together. My strongest memory was of the humble monument on the site of the first QANTAS office, so significant to our aviation history, but so easily passed without notice. For a moment I recalled standing at the edge of the paddock where Houdini had first flown and another moment in history oft overlooked.

Similarly, Winton passes beneath my nose at two miles per minute and is gone in a moment, but not forgotten. An hour later, I overfly Julia Creek and another forty minutes later, Cloncurry is ticked off the flight plan. In my modern cockpit they are mere waypoints, but in reality, Julia Creek was the destination and Cloncurry the origin of the first official flight of the Royal Flying Doctor Service.

John Flynn had previously experimented with the concept of an aerial inland mission having witnessed the tragedies that had befallen the outback's pioneers for lack of medical care. In time his experiment grew, and in 1928 he had the finances to launch the entity that would ultimately become the globally-renowned Royal Flying Doctor Service. One of his supporters was the QANTAS founder, Hudson Fysh, and the first aircraft was also supplied by the airline. These two quintessentially Australian organisations were linked from birth and even today the QANTAS Foundation supports the work of the RFDS.

For a lover of aviation and history, these miles beneath me are golden. I can almost see the ancient DH50 biplane leaving its trail of dust below as it lumbers into the sky on another selfless mission of mercy. I can hear the roar of the engine and see the pilot in his open cockpit weathering the elements while his precious human cargo remained shelter within the cabin ahead of him. I tip my hat to those who had the courage to see their vision through to reality without any of the creature comforts that we enjoy today.

From Cloncurry I set a westerly course to Mount Isa. For a while I share the company of a mining train that is seemingly endless with its carriages full of ore. The Isa is far more familiar to me, having flown here only weeks before, albeit in a Boeing 737. From a good distance out, I sight the chimneys and the ridgeline to the west of the airport. Isa is a thriving mining town with regular jet services and all manner of light aircraft launching for smaller outback stations. I monitor the radio carefully and coordinate my arrival with the comings and goings of this busy airport.

A strong wind is blowing down Runway 16 as I line up for the landing. There is a little convective turbulence bouncing me around as the day warms up, but mostly I am struck by my slow speed over the ground as I approach to land. Gradually the runway draws closer, and finally I arrive over the bitumen where I hover onto the surface with just a trickle of forward speed. I keep the power on a touch and accelerate toward the next turnoff to clear the runway for the inbound aeroplanes I can hear chattering on the radio.

The Jabiru with my other 'office' in the background at Mount Isa

Friendly folks and family at The Isa

As I pull the Jabiru up to the fuel bowser, there is a small gathering of people. Most are from the local base of the RFDS, on hand to give me a welcome, and the other is a reporter from the ABC. It is always touching to be met by welcoming faces no matter how far from home you may be. My website and the media tell me that people are following the flight, but the chance to stop and chat and put faces to the ISP addresses is so much more. After a brief conversation, it emerges that I am related to one of the RFDS staff; my father and her grandfather were cousins!

They had shared a rather 'Tom Sawyer' upbringing on the Darling Downs during the 1930s. It was the hard times of the Great Depression and drought on the land, and yet these young boys made the most of their childhood. Undoubtedly, their tough upbringing served them well as their manhood was destined to be overshadowed by a world at war, hurling them to all corners of the globe. Here I was, miles from anywhere and yet, again, Dad has poked his nose into this flight around Australia.

I am given the grand tour of the RFDS facility and their Super King Airs, whose interior aeromedical kit-out is particularly interesting to me as both a pilot and a former paramedic. The good people even have a cake to mark my visit to Mount Isa, and I could spend a lot more time here chatting about family and flying. However, by the time I have completed the media interviews, the clock is ticking loudly, and the trusty Jabiru is ready to take me across my first state border.

For the first time, a real sense of isolation struck me. With Mount Isa's chimneys shrinking to matchsticks behind me, very little lies ahead. The road and rail line roughly parallel my route to serve as a comforting back-up to my navigation, but otherwise there is only mile upon mile of vast expanse. One by one, the bars indicating the signal strength of my mobile phone drop away until the phone is little more than a camera and an inert box of circuitry. Still, it continues to hunt for some trace of communication with the outside world. Searching, searching....

The towering clouds ahead begin to dump their watery contents in a series of rain showers that are too opaque to penetrate. As I skirt the edges, the occasional spray reaches the Jabiru as if to wipe its face and quench its thirst with the temperature climbing into the thirties. All around me, the green tinge continues to colour the outback and usually dry creek beds boast water and billabongs. This rain is obviously not the first of the year.

Camooweal and its population of a few hundred people emerge from behind a shower with the Barkly Highway running into it like a yellow brick road. My GPS, map, and the world outside are in total agreement as the clock ticks over right on time. I had mentioned Camooweal in my live radio interview back at Mount Isa, so I take a few moments to lazily circle the town in a gentle arc. Sure enough, people emerge from their homes and looked skyward at the little

Jabiru overhead, waving the occasional tea towel. It was a heart-warming moment that didn't end when I rolled the aircraft level and continued on my way to Barkly Homestead.

Downtown Camooweal

11

DISTANT VOICES.

Long Shadows at Barkly

Day Two. Barkly Homestead.

Minutes after I depart Camooweal, I leave Queensland and enter the Northern Territory. There are no dotted lines on the ground to confirm the fact, just a reminder on the moving map of my GPS.

The Barkly Highway stretches out ahead as I enter my fifth and final hour of flight time for the day. Buzz Aldrin once described the lunar surface as "magnificent desolation", and while there is still vegetation below, I can understand to some degree what he meant. There is a real beauty in a vastness void of man. It makes one feel so small and insignificant, and yet can inspire the mind to a deeper level of reflection. Perhaps it brushes away the illusion of self-importance and offers a sense of perspective in its place. Whatever it is, I draw a deep breath and smile at the remote world around me.

Gradually, the earth becomes redder and the green tinges sparser. Only the occasional bore breaks the trend like an outback oasis. The highway comes back toward me, and if I allowed my eye to follow its thin black line, I can just see a small group of buildings, but little more. It is Barkly Homestead and that isolated gathering is to be my home for the night.

An Outback Bore

I nose the Jabiru over into a speedy descent, partly for efficiency and partly out of an enthusiasm to land. The red dirt runway is not far from the road with a thin track seeming to join it to the greater community. As I join the landing circuit overhead, I struggle to interpret the windsock which appears to be hanging very limply. There are no water masses, trees, smoke, or flags to offer any telltale signs of the wind direction or strength either. It is strange that the conditions are so calm when I had been enjoying a very healthy tailwind for the last half an hour.

Nevertheless, given the conditions I decide to land toward the settlement, so after landing I can simply taxi off into town without having to backtrack down the runway. I position the aircraft to land, but as I enter the final stages of the approach it is obvious that conditions are not calm at all. I can sense the aircraft drifting sidewards over the ground on the base leg, pushing me toward the airfield. Then as I turn to line up with the runway, the picture outside isn't correct and it is apparent that there is a tailwind pushing me at speed toward the runway.

I decide to abort the landing attempt and fly a 'missed approach'. As I pass the windsock at this lower altitude, it becomes obvious why it was hanging limply; there is virtually nothing left of it. Just a few shreds of cloth hang from the ring at the top of the pole, offering no worthwhile information about the wind speed or direction. As aircraft are designed to ideally land into wind, I reverse my intended landing and proceeded to touchdown on the fine red silt of Barkly Homestead's runway without any further drama.

This windsock had very little left to say.

Taxiing from the airstrip into town is an adventure in its own right. It is not so much a taxiway built for aeroplanes as a track built for four-wheel drives. The surface is far from level, and the undergrowth reaches out from either side. I maintain a slow pace, conscious of not striking the propeller and watching each wing tip in turn to avoid banging into a branch. It is challenging, but I love it! This is outback flying. This is the flying of my youth.

I emerge from the scrub into a clearing where a lone fuel bowser stands ready to fill the Jabiru's thirsty tanks. When the propeller comes to a halt, I pause for a few minutes to complete the paperwork, sign off the flight details, and take in the scenery around me. I climb out and pop Bert onto the engine cowling to pose for a photo for my children, while I wait to see if anyone emerges from the buildings over yonder.

Bert takes a breather at Barkly.

As I wipe down the Jabiru's flanks like a sweaty mare, I am met by one of the locals with a shake of the hand and an iconic "G'Day". He assists me in getting the fuel pump started as it was being cantankerous and didn't want to start. After a nudge here and there, the pump motor begins to hum, and I fill the Jabiru with fuel as kite-hawks sweep in circles overhead.

I am directed to a parking spot near the caravans, but the track looks a touch too narrow for me, so I opt to pull the Jabiru by hand to its resting place for the night. Dragging the aircraft by its propeller, it bobbles and bounces along the uneven track as I contemplate a shower and a hot meal. Finally, I have the aircraft parked and unpacked, by which time a small crowd of interested onlookers have arrived to see the aeroplane in the midst of their cabins and trailers. Despite feeling decidedly weary, I show several people the Jabiru and explain the purpose of my flight. As always, the Royal Flying Doctor Service crest and motto on the aircraft provided a central starting point for the questions.

As the crowd dwindles, I check into my cabin for the night. It is a simple, clean and tidy demountable building and just as I remember it from my stay here with my father twenty years before. In fact, the very cabin we stayed in is a mere two doors away and, once again, a strong sense of sentiment runs through me. However, it was not the time to idly ponder just yet as I still have phone interviews to conduct, blogs to write, and emails to answer. Only then can I sign off the day behind me and ready for the one ahead.

The night is almost upon Barkly and the wind is beginning to die down. The colours of the sunset beyond the water tower are amazing, and I decide to farewell the day in silence beside the Jabiru. The last rays of light subside, and I enjoy the warm, dark silence a little longer.

Finally, I head across to the restaurant where some good outback fare is on the menu. Steaks that could have been cut from dinosaurs and all you can eat salads, vegetables, and chips. The Irish waitress that takes my order tells me how she is working her way around Australia and this outback whistle-stop was her latest destination. I admire her free will but couldn't help thinking of the gulf that exists between Belfast and Barkly.

The end of the day at Barkly Homestead

Back in my room, I make one last call home to Kirrily and the kids before turning in. In the absence of streetlights, the room is pitch black with the silence only occasionally broken by a passing Road Train or wildlife scratching around in the scrub outside. My mind steps through time as I recall the last time I had rested at Barkly on another dark, dark night. It was an evening that I have never forgotten.

It was set to the soundtrack of my father's breathing; rhythmic, deep, and gradually slowing. Yet despite his fatigue from the day's driving, sleep was not forthcoming, and eventually his voice moved bodiless about the room. The sound of his creaking bed gave way to steady pacing as he moved unseen. This very quiet man stopped and then began to speak in a way that I have never heard.

Made anonymous by the night, he spoke of a childhood of hard times and the shame of a farm lost. He spoke of war, blood, and death. Hour after hour, my father delved deeper and deeper into his soul as I lay awkwardly in silence. He jumped from the steamy the jungles of New Guinea and a patrol gone wrong, to the frigid hills of Korea and the devastation he witnessed at Hiroshima. The recollections were only interrupted when he offered up answers to questions I would never dare ask. His mood swung between acceptance and raging hate and only when the clock passed 2 a.m. did the pace subside to infrequent muttering before he finally lay down and his breathing slowed into sleep. I had not said a single word.

Now I lie alone, two rooms and twenty years from that night. I have often wondered if he knew then that he was dying and felt a need to purge his being of those things that had never been uttered. I will never know, although I have my suspicions. For him, his journey was nearing its end that night at Barkly. For me, I still have so far to go.

Barkly Sunset

12

A Hornet's Nest.

Hornet Head-On

Day Three. Barkly Homestead – Katherine – Darwin.

I rise early once again, having slept deeply for every minute. My memories have never haunted me or stirred me from sleep. Even as a nineteen-year-old paramedic, I was able to stow those images best forgotten and carry on with life as I knew it and my recollections of my father at Barkly that night was no exception.

I consume some cereal and fruit, sling my kit bag over my shoulder, and make my way by torchlight across Barkly to the waiting Jabiru. Cool, dark and quiet. These moments before dawn are magical. I unlash the aircraft from its lodgings and load my gear on board. Getting creative, I set up my tripod and camera to record my preflight routine once the sun has risen. Slowly as the daylight arrived, it became obvious that I was no actor.

First my attempts to film my preflight inspection are thwarted by poor camera positioning and then pushing the aircraft into the clearing takes four attempts as it was sitting in slight gully. All I captured up to that point was some quality footage of me acquiring a hernia. Finally, the filming starts to take shape, and once again the crowd has gathered to watch the lone pilot and his little aeroplane. Once again, I pull the Jabiru a few hundred yards through the fine dirt and eroded ridges to a safe place to start the engine and get underway.

As I creep back along the dirt track to the runway, the Jabiru's elongated shadow keeps me company and I pass the shredded windsock one more time. It doesn't matter now as the early morning is without the slightest puff of a breeze. The long trek has given the engine more than adequate time to warm up, so after the final pre-takeoff checks, I open the throttle and get day three underway. As I depart overhead, I can still see the small gathering of folks below waving goodbye. I waggled the wings in recognition of their well wishes and head for the Royal Australian Air Force base at Katherine; RAAF Tindal.

With the sun and wind at my back, it is a four-hour sector across to Tindal. After the first hour, I chew on another muesli bar and turn the Jabiru from west to a more northerly heading over Tennant Creek. Here, just out of town, there is a memorial to the late Reverend John Flynn, the founder of the RFDS, but other than that there is very little to interrupt the endless scenery ahead. Lake Woods passes down the left-hand side, boasting a substantial amount of water, while the hamlet of Elliott and its mandatory airstrip sits to the north. Onwards I fly with the highway never very distant, passing through Daly Waters, Mataranka, and Elsey Station where the book, "We of the Never Never" was set and many of its characters are now at rest.

Elliott, Northern Territory

Out of radio range to receive the latest weather reports, the marvel of modern technology of the iPhone allows me to still access the conditions and runway in use at Tindal. I had organised my arrival at the RAAF base well in advance, as a special clearance was required at this joint military-civil installation. The Air Force has been very helpful throughout the process and we even exchanged some photos in the preceding weeks. For RAAF Tindal is home to Australia's No. 75 Squadron, flying the FA-18 Hornet fighter jet. By coincidence, yet again, my father had served with 75 Squadron for a period flying somewhat older fighters than those that now tear up the skies over Katherine.

Jock Thompson Phil Zupp Trevor Killian Max Holdsworth
75 Sqn-- Williamtown--c1955

While the weather is fine, my descent into Tindal provides me with the first real turbulence of the trip. It is now late morning and as the day warms up, invisible heated parcels of air begin to rise into the atmosphere. These rising bubbles bump and bounce the Jabiru around unkindly so I slow down to minimise the jolting on the airframe. Even so, the buffeting continues as I manoeuvre to land with one eye on the runway and the other enviously surveying the impressive line-up of Hornet fighters.

Over the fence at Tindal

On the ground, my first port of call is the fuel bowser, and then a group of sixty school-children who have come to see the Jabiru and hear a little about the history of flight in Australia. They already know a great deal about the Flying Doctors. It is an enjoyable hour chatting with the kids, even if they throw me questions out of left-field such as, "Where's the toilet?" Taking time to spread the word of aviation among potential pilots of the future is an important part of the flight, but as the minutes ticked away, I still have another appointment with the RAAF and the rest of the day's flying to Darwin.

A great group of kids at Tindal

By the time I arrive on the Air Force's side of the airfield, I am running late. Sadly, the Chief of the Air Force, Air Marshall Mark Binskin had just departed, but there was still a tremendous turn-out by the RAAF. Not only have they conveniently parked a Hornet for a photo opportunity, but these central Australian service personnel have passed the hat around at the front gate and raised $500 for the RFDS. As a farewell gift, I receive an official 75 Squadron 'Magpie' patch and a drink cooler that I will undoubtedly use when the day is over.

I am overwhelmed by both the reception and the generosity at Tindal, but it is time to go. With the day growing older, the turbulence will also be growing in strength. Once again, the road winds its way northward, and so do I. The flight is not as rough as I had anticipated as I settle in for the run into Darwin. Thirsty as always, I continually hydrate by drinking copious amounts of water, and yet the Katherine's schoolchildren's fears never eventuate, and a toilet isn't needed in flight.

The Jabiru is in fine company with this 75 Squadron Hornet.

The township of Batchelor comes and goes, but not without notice. During World War Two it had been a major Air Force base and a strategic element in the defence of Australia. In fact, the further north I fly, the more old airstrips became apparent. Scratched into the scrub and generally not far from the road, these forgotten runways had once provided a place to land for aircraft ranging from bombers to the classic Spitfire fighters. Now I overfly them in far more peaceful skies.

Further north, the state's capital of Darwin is my rich in even more distant aviation history.

For Darwin was Australia's northern outpost where those first pioneer aviators first made landfall on their flights from Mother England. Sir Ross and Keith Smith, Bert Hinkler and even Amelia Earhart transited the Northern Territory's capital. I ponder that thought for the moment and check my top pocket where Hinkler's autograph is carefully stowed.

The turbulence I anticipated may not have been forthcoming, but now the visibility begins to decrease as the air about me fills with smoke. May is a prime month for controlled 'burn-offs' in the Northern Territory and now that smoke is all around me. Between the GPS and good old-fashioned map reading, I carefully steer my course and ready to enter the Darwin's controlled airspace. With so many people following the flight on the internet I am very careful to fly by-the-book, and I don't want to inadvertently penetrate airspace without permission, even if the visibility was poor.

From Batchelor I track via Manton Dam and, fifteen minutes later, the air is clear, and Darwin lies dead ahead. Like Mount Isa, Darwin was no stranger to me as I often fly the Boeing there, but the approach to land is far tighter when you're in a two-seat Jabiru. In a matter of minutes, I am on the ground after nearly six hours of flight time. As always, I refuel and unpack the Jabiru, only this time I am met by the Lord Mayor of Darwin, Mr Graeme Sawyer. Not a small man, he is keen to try the Jabiru on for size and climbs aboard to get a feel for the cockpit.

The Lord Mayor of Darwin tries on the Jabiru for size.

We chatted for quite some time before I finally make my way beyond the airport fence where I meet John Zupp for the first time. He has kindly offered to drive me to my hotel room which wasn't far away, but it would be a long-haul with my gear at the end of a taxing day. We speak about the flight and work out how we are related. It turns out that his grandfather was my father's uncle and had lost his leg in France during World War One.

Back in my room the daily routine of flight planning, blogging and phone interviews is supplemented by a load of laundry. I send a photo of Bert to the kids and call them before a good meal of Chinese food and still even more iced water. My day is over, and I lie down, falling straight into a deep sleep.

Bert relaxing at the end of a long day.

Then my world erupts when the phone rings beside my head. Thinking it was a wake-up call, I sit bolt upright before realising that it was not the hotel phone, but my mobile phone. My heart racing with the surge of adrenalin, I answer the incoming call from a number I don't recognise. It is Flight Service, querying a detail on the next day's flight plan. I gather my thoughts and provide them with the information they require before hanging up and looking at the clock. It wasn't wake-up time...it was midnight. Ugh!

13

A Blast from the Past.

Day Four. Darwin – Kununurra.

Despite the midnight call, I wake up surprisingly rested, although the world outside is dark and still. I have been looking forward to this day ever since I began planning the solo flight around Australia. Some of my most enjoyable flying had been as a young charter pilot finding my way around the beautiful Kimberley region of Australia. Today I am going to retrace some of my fledgling aviator steps, and my final check of the day's weather suggests that the scene will be set to the backdrop of gloriously blue skies.

Breakfast again consists of cereal, juice, and this time the bonus of burnt toast. One side effect of solo flying, compared to airline operations, is a noticeable weight loss. Having settled my account the night before, I walk through the empty hotel foyer and along the deserted airport roads to where the Jabiru is parked. Even though the sun is yet to rise, the heat and humidity has already begun to stir, and I pause momentarily to lower my heavy bags and flick the sweat off my forehead.

On the tarmac, the Jabiru sits in silence, but not for long, as the cranking of engines and the glare of aircraft lights begin to fill the air. The day begins early for a pilot in the Top End, with pre-dawn departures being the norm. To the same backdrop that I had witnessed many years before, I load up the Jabiru and begin another long day with more than six hours of flight time ahead of me.

Pre-Dawn at Darwin

Climbing away, the morning sun now rises to my left as I set course to the south for the first time on this journey. The air traffic controllers are very accommodating. They clear me straight out in the direction of Port Keats and wish me well as I leave their airspace and radio frequency bound for Kununurra.

It is just like old times as I make my way across the marshy low lands toward Keats, where the familiar airstrip emerges not far from the coast on the Bonaparte Gulf. I had been into Port Keats many times before, carrying cargo and local indigenous Australians, with whom I came to know by name and share a joke. Leo Melpi and Harry Ginger come to mind, and a smile widens across my face as I look down at the settlement.

Port Keats ahead

I climb up to 6,500 feet before I look to cross the Gulf and track via Quoin Island. The theory was to always remain within gliding distance of land, given the shark and crocodile-infested nature of the waters below. And while I am confident of the gliding performance of the lightweight, streamlined Jabiru I'm flying today, I can't help but think I may have been a little naive as a youngster in my heavily laden Cessna 210 or 206. Thankfully, I was never called upon to find out whether I would have made landfall all those years ago, although I get a shiver now just thinking about it.

The scenery below me feels so familiar, despite the passage of time. The mud flats with the vein-like waterways branching out beyond their edges into the green, low-lying lands that border the gulf. Here I sit in the clearest of blue skies, passing through the same piece of air that I traversed as a young pilot. They were golden times and in my mind's eye I can still see the other Cessnas as we fly in a loose formation back to Kununurra. We didn't have two cents to our name, but those were some of the most wonderful days of flying over the amazing canvas that is The Kimberleys.

As Kununurra nears, the irrigation scheme to the north of the town boasts the rich greens of fruit plantations, seemingly incongruous in this outback realm. The small red towers of beehive-like rock formations to the east mark the Hidden Valley, where I once lived in a caravan, while the Ord River skirts the airport to the west on its way to Lake Argyle. It is all so vivid, I feel like I am coming home as I turn the Jabiru onto the downwind leg of the circuit in preparation of landing.

Landfall over the Bonaparte Gulf

The film camera beside me is capturing the images as I slide down my final approach, over The Ord with the Diversion Dam out to the right. The security of the asphalt rumbles beneath my wheels before too long and I exit the runway to immediately be greeted by a modern passenger terminal, flanked by towering palm trees. Our old hangar still stands, but under new ownership. My old company, Slingair, is located in one of a series of new buildings, and there is one very familiar aeroplane; my old Cessna 310, VH-TWY.

I draw to a halt and park the Jabiru along the same tie-down cables where I would once load my passengers before dawn and the Kimberley heat arrived. Today is mild at 29 degrees, with just a light breeze and none of the coastal humidity; perfect. I step out of the cockpit and wander past the lines of aircraft and buildings toward the Slingair office where I'm greeted by a friendly smile and a free bottle of ice-cold water.

The Jabiru parked on my old home turf at Kununurra

The surroundings have come a long way in twenty years, as have the security gates and fences. I ask if I can have a close-up look at their

Cessna 310 that I used to fly two decades ago, and I am met with two reactions. One reaction was of wonder by the receptionist who wasn't born then and another of disbelief, bordering on horror, that they had an aircraft that was that old. I felt that I had asked for a guided tour of the Ark...and I was Noah!

Nevertheless, they escorted me out to VH-TWY, or 'Twiggy' as I called her. There she stood, those familiar lines, now coated in another few layers of peeling paint. As a new commercial pilot, Twiggy had been a big step up. Two engines, 180 knots, and sleek lines dominated by a pair of massive, pointed fuel tanks on each wing tip. I used to sit in that cockpit and feel like I was sitting atop a magic carpet.

Those fuel tanks on her wings did not lend her to scenic flying, so Twiggy and I would venture to remote destinations and airstrips of red silt instead. All the way down to Perth on occasions, eight hours and three stops to take burly miners home to the city. We had shared some exciting moments, too. There was day that I nearly stopped both engines as I emptied the auxiliary tanks a little too much and was a little too slow moving the fuel selector. Then there was the time that a magneto on the left-hand engine imploded and I diverted into Meekatharra on one engine where I was subsequently marooned for a couple of days. They were good times and a steep learning curve.

I so wanted to stay a night in Kununurra, but part of me also knew that it would be very different. For all its raw Australian beauty, it was the people that made my time in the Kimberleys a period of my life that I would forever treasure. And the fact was that those days had moved on and a whole new generation of keen young pilots were now making their own mistakes and memories. Now I was just some old guy with great stories behind me, but still many miles ahead of me. It was time to leave Kununurra and my youth and set course for the coast.

My old girl, "Twiggy"

14

BARE BEAUTY AND BROOME.

Beautiful Broome

Day Four. Kununurra – Broome.

As I banked overhead Kununurra to set course and depart, I surveyed my surroundings one last time. My eye was drawn to the Diversion Dam where water was dribbling over the wall. It was here that on my first day in Kununurra, Dad's slouch hat had blown from his head and into the waters below. A survivor from his Air Force days it now became as one with the Ord River. At first Dad made moves to head the hat off at a point downstream, but then he stopped." You know..." he started, "...if it has to meet its end after all these years, that's not a bad way to go." He smiled and then leaned back on the railing, surveying the churning water and the disappearing headgear below. As I flew overhead today the water wasn't churning below me, but I swear that I could almost see that hat.

The Ord River wound its way toward Lake Argyle and with every turn in the river, another memory was evoked, including the day I came across a Special Forces landing party during a major military exercise. And then there was the Ord Top Dam that marked the threshold of the massive Lake Argyle. I was flying over this very dam wall when I ticked over the first thousand hours in my log book.

The magic of Lake Argyle

The beauty of Lake Argyle is nothing new to me as I flew around one hundred scenic flights over its vast expanse on the way to the Bungle Bungle Ranges. Even so, the sight takes my breath away today just as it did back then. Like an enormous inland sea, the lake extends to the horizon with the occasional island jutting up from its blue-green waters. Once at the mercy of the seasonal changes between 'the wet' and 'the dry', this fresh-water supply now covers 900 square kilometres of Kimberley earth. And despite the marketing to tourists and the freshwater contained within her banks, I have seen huge salt-water crocodiles sunning themselves on the banks of Lake Argyle.

The enormity and wealth of the Argyle Diamond Mine is impressive.

As the southern tip of the lake approaches, the scenery becomes dominated by the Argyle Diamond Mine. One of the world's most productive diamond mines, its open cut nature has gradually chewed off the end of the mountain range. The sheer amount of the earth that has been moved since the mine opened in 1985 has to be seen to be believed and in that time around 800 million carats of diamonds have been mined. I survey the scene, feeling very small, and wonder how many Jabirus I could buy with that many diamonds.

I am only half an hour out of Kununurra, and as I turn westward, I still have the best part of four hours to go. The land ahead is remote, really remote. It is the vast northwest and not much exists out here on a permanent basis. I have flown through this region many times, but the first thing that strikes me now is the greenness of the surrounding scenery. The dry creek beds that I remember are now filled with water and the clumps of undergrowth have become a green carpet with foliage rising in every direction. The earth looks healthy and well quenched as I slip along briskly in the smoothest of Kimberley air toward Mount House.

Looking around, I wonder how far away the next living soul may be, comforted by my emergency beacon and Spidertracks system should I be forced down out here. Yet for a moment, I don't think about being forced down; what if I was to land? The occasional clearing beside the river banks is almost seductive in offering of a safe place to land. I have landed on worse. Like a siren's call, the thought of parking the Jabiru in the middle of nowhere and breathing in the outback at close range is a wondrous thought. But that is all it is.

Making my way across the Kimberleys with a healthy tailwind

The reality is that out here, you don't take chances. That enticing paddock by the water could be filled with barbs, ready to deflate your tyres. Those picturesque river banks are an ideal location, not just for the weary traveller, but possibly a stray crocodile. And what if the dream of a peaceful break was realised and then the Jabiru's engine failed to start? What then? I dream for a moment more before slapping myself back to the real world and scanning ahead for the King Leopold Ranges.

Amongst the King Leopold Ranges

Mount House

The terrain begins to flatten out further, losing its undulations. In their place, the occasional mesa-like formation rises from the floor below, one of which is Mount House. A little ahead of time, I pass overhead the small cluster of buildings that constitutes Mount House Station with its standard-issue red-dirt airstrip. This is cattle country and the cattle stations are big. Someone back in Kununurra told me that Mount House Station was 1.5 million acres and looking around; I don't doubt it.

Broome is still over an hour away; I tally the fuel used since Kununurra and project the fuel that will remain at Broome. To date, the Jabiru has been performing better than my conservative flight planning figures, and I calculate that I'll still have more than an hour's fuel on board when I touchdown at the day's end. For a moment, I entertain landing at Derby to stretch my legs and top up the tanks, but with the tailwind still pushing me along at a good pace, I decide to maintain my altitude and cruise home for the final stages.

Below me, the landscape begins to change as the inland gives way to the coastal fringe. First, rocky outcrops begin to jut up on a broad scale, replacing the landing-friendly terrain of the last couple of hours. These gnarly little hillocks seem to stand like an igneous fence line before the tidal mudflats appear ahead and Derby comes into view. Just another fifty minutes to go.

For the first time on this flight, the Australian west coast and the Indian Ocean come into view. Its blue tones on the horizon are only slightly obscured by more smoke from yet more burning off, but even so, there is no mistaking it. For the time being, I have left the inland behind me and now cosy coastal navigation will be my guide. I have yet another drink of water and organise my cockpit and cameras for the arrival into Broome. Once again, this is one of my ports of call in the 737, so I'm not only familiar with the airfield, but I recognise the friendly voice over the radio. It is a comforting end to a long but wondrous day.

Derby Airport and the tidal mudflats

I have beaten the peak hour rush of the arriving airliners, but I keep my speed up as I know they are not far behind. The ever-reliable Jabiru responds to my call and the world whizzes by underneath as the runway sweeps past to one side. I begin to decelerate and raise the nose, waiting for the speed to wash off so that I can begin lowering flap. I am struck by the stunningly white sands edging the most crystal-clear waters you could ever imagine. As I roll into a turn a short distance off the coast, I can see straight down through the water to the soft sand on the ocean's floor. I am entranced by the purity of the scene below me such that it takes a genuine effort to re-focus on the task at hand.

Flying abeam the runway at beautiful Broome; not long to go now

The whir of the motors and the slow-moving indicator in the corner of my eye remind me that the flaps are being lowered and the end of my day is near. The airspeed sits steady and the Jabiru rests lightly under the control of my hand as the beach, and then the road, and then the runway's edge pass beneath my wheels. They touch down on the rough runway surface almost in protest that such a flight should end. But so it must.

By the time the Jabiru has fallen silent on the apron, it is overshadowed by the string of jets announcing their arrival with the roar of reverse thrust. The shining red QANTAS tail is a shade brighter in the west coast sun, and I even feel a touch of pride in the flying kangaroo as it exits the runway on the 'big boy's' side of the airport. I am proud, but not envious, as I haul my gear beyond the airport perimeter to stand in the shade of a hangar and wait for a taxi. For I have been intimate with the terrain these last few days, not looking down from on high in the flight levels. I have felt every contour and studied the shadows cast by trees on the river banks. Communities have looked up and waved and I have waggled my wings back at them in a mutual "G'day."

The Jabiru takes a well-earned rest at Broome.

By the time I have checked into the hotel behind two busloads of tourists, I confess to being tired and hungry. There is a message on my phone showing my son taking his first steps and my heart sinks at having missed the moment. I share a wonderful phone call with

Kirrily and the kids, but the truth is that it just isn't the same. This is the only time I have questioned whether it is all worth the effort. However, I know that it is only the distance from my family and the fatigue of my body and mind playing games with my spirit.

I shake myself from the malaise and complete the day's interviews, email my reports to the newspapers, and fine-tune the flight planning for the next day. With everything completed, I consume the world's largest room service hamburger and a slab of nutritious chocolate cake, washed down with ice-cold lemonade. I have gained an hour and a half of daylight when I crossed the border into Western Australia, so the day is far from over as I darken my room and slip between the sheets.

Long days, fresh air, and clean living make for a good night's sleep and that was exactly what Broome delivered to my room that night. For ten hours, I didn't move a muscle until the alarm clock interrupted my hibernation. When my eyes opened the room was still dark, but my enthusiasm was back in full swing as I leap out of bed.

Today is to be the longest day's flying of the entire journey, so I showered and gathered my gear without a wasted moment. I carefully closed the hotel room door with a quiet 'click', so as not to wake the other residents, and slid my key and account under the door at Reception. As the taxi's headlights swept into the driveway, there was still no inkling of dawn and I marvelled at the sea of stars overhead, unimpeded in the absence of city lights. This was going to be a day to remember.

15

THE RED EARTH.

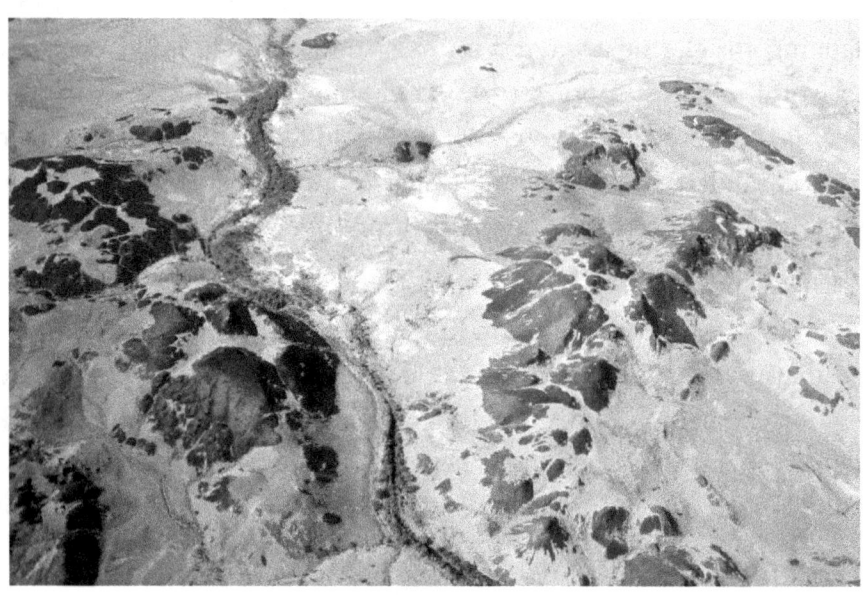

The remote Pilbara

Day Five. Broome – Port Hedland – Carnarvon.

Pre-dawn on a Sunday morning tends to be a quiet hour on the streets of Broome. Into the mix is the fact that today is Mother's Day and deserving ladies across the nation have no intention of opening their eyes for a good while yet. As we make our way to the airport, I strike up a conversation with the young taxi driver, who, by coincidence, knows all about my flight around Australia. And who, by a greater coincidence, is a young commercial pilot waiting in Broome for his first big break into the aviation industry.

I sit there, captivated by his unbridled enthusiasm, and I could be looking in a mirror whose light takes twenty-five years to bounce back. With eight hours and nearly a thousand miles ahead of me, this young pilot sharing his dreams is the perfect way for my day to start. When we pull up outside the darkened airport, he is out of the car like a flash, carrying the heaviest of my bags to the Jabiru. We continue to chat as I load the aeroplane, while the first rays of light sneakily begin to glow over the inland to the east. As he turns to leave, I prepare to hand over my fare with a generous tip when the young aviator waves it away in protest. He insists that it was his pleasure to drive me to the airport and if I am committed to getting rid of my money, then I can donate it to the RFDS like the other good folks. Without further fanfare, he walks away leaving me standing alone but filled with admiration.

With daylight now available to illuminate the aeroplane, I begin my daily inspection of the Jabiru. As I approach the tail, a little bird lands on the fin and sits there staring at me, unfazed by the lumbering upright mammal in the baseball cap. As I continue to walk around the aeroplane, his relaxed manner impresses me, and I wonder if inside he is laughing at this human being who is about to mimic flight using combustion and horsepower. Then, as silently as he had arrived, he springs from his perch and flies gracefully into the remaining shreds of darkness and again, I was left standing alone but filled with admiration.

A fellow aviator watches my preflight inspection at Broome.

By the time I have arranged my cockpit, strapped in, and brought the Jabiru to life, the sun is beginning to emerge. Like the roads, the airport is deserted, and I transmit my radio calls blindly into the atmosphere as if someone might hear. The empty skies above and the hum of the warming, rhythmic engine is a perfect combination to welcome in the day. With everything in order, I enter the runway facing east, smoothly advance the throttle and begin to run at the sun.

As the nosewheel lifts off and the ground falls away, I climb toward the sun's rays over the curving horizon. Ever so steadily, the glowing day becomes a fierce red ball with its first shards of light stabbing at my sunglasses. The air is still, and the beautiful colours of the previous afternoon take on a different hue. The blues and whites are more sedate, as if they too are easing into the day and yet they are no less majestic; if anything, a little more so. It is a 'great to be alive' moment as I gently nudge around the sandy shores and climb into clear skies.

A stunning sunrise as I depart Broome

This is my first 'beach flying' of the flight and I revel in the ease of navigation and the security of limitless places to land. As the sun continues to rise, the colours of the world below transition into a new spectrum and the long shadows of dawn are replaced by the finer details of the terrain. Aqua waters blend into broad strips of white sand which, in turn, give way to low scrub and undergrowth. The further south I fly, the more isolated these idyllic beaches become.

After an hour, Sandfire Road passes beneath and serves as a convenient check-point halfway to Port Hedland. Still the occasional airstrip is scratched out into the scrub for a remote community, a mine site or a long-forgotten squadron from a war so long ago. Everywhere that I have flown, these lines in the sand have been evidence of aviation's critical role in supporting the distant reaches of Australia. A life-line to a small population stretched over a vast land.

Before the airport at Port Hedland comes into view, a series of large white squares on the coast contrast with the surrounding greens and browns of the surrounding land. As I draw closer it becomes evident that these are vast evaporative ponds used to 'farm' salt from the nearby sea-water. It is a major operation with huge ocean-going vessels at anchor in port just beyond the salt farms. I pass overhead the white grid as I position to land and with minutes I am back on the ground and taxiing in for my first fuel stop for the day.

The last time I was at Port Hedland, I had diverted there in a Boeing when dreadful weather enveloped the entire west coast. That day we just managed to get below the cloud base and land, but my strongest memory is the wind. Howling at a phenomenal speed, it drove the low overcast as if I was viewing a slice of time-lapse photography. That day the refuelling agent scratched his head at the sight of a 737 at his airport and left me to climb the ladder, switch the valves, and pump the juice into the long, swept wings. Today, the sky is cloudless, and the airport deserted.

Port Hedland waters off the wingtip

The control tower has fallen silent since my last visit and now sits there in ghostly isolation. A few aircraft are out on the tarmac, the terminal building is empty and all but one of the hangars has its doors closed. I park at the bowser and wonder where I can find a bathroom to dump my own fuel. I wander to the sole open hangar and find a lone sign of life, lying on his back and cleaning the belly of an aeroplane. We trade greetings and pleasantries and the absence of commercial aviation, particularly here and today at Port Hedland. I comment that the fact it is Mother's Day is probably a contributing factor on such a sunny Sunday. The words were no sooner out of my mouth than my friend rolled from under his aircraft and stood bolt upright, swearing as he moved in one fluent motion. Without another word he abandoned the hangar and ran to his car, leaving a trail of dust in his wake. I only hope he was forgiven for obviously forgetting Mother's Day.

Alone again, I attend to my business and check the latest weather. The next stop is Carnarvon and it is four hours away, so I ensure that my food and water is all within easy reach. For this sector I have planned inland over the rich mining region of the Pilbara as I 'cut the corner' on the Australian coastline. Sitting in the aircraft, I run my finger along the route on my chart and appreciate that the miles ahead are just a step when compared to the enormity of this country. However, it is far from daunting and I smile in anticipation of the continuing adventure as the Jabiru's propeller swings back into life and the now familiar checklists recommence.

I lift off toward the east before heading south, skirting the western edge of the Hamersley Ranges, and some distance from the big mining centres of Tom Price and Paraburdoo. Immediately, the coastal fringe with its vegetation falls away to my right, and the landscape becomes characterised by increasingly rich reds and ochre tones. The flat lands of the coast are also lost as the terrain begins to alternate between undulating hills and ragged rising ranges. In between, strips of green hug the banks of a water course that weaves its way through the Pilbara.

People are few and far between out here. Hardy aboriginal communities have survived for centuries, while the white Europeans tend to congregate about the mine sites with their vast wealth of iron ore. Dark red hills, bordering on being black, rise from the silt and surrounds. Everywhere that I look there are signs of long past violent volcanic activity, side-by-side with more recent erosion and gently worn knolls.

The rugged red ranges of the Pilbara

This raw beauty is awe-inspiring, and I only wish I could look down from above at the tiny, clean, white Jabiru set against this expansive red blanket. To see its tiny, ivory wings tracing an invisible line across a region that is traversed so infrequently. My aircraft and I are so insignificant compared to breadth and history of this amazing land. We are but a blip on the radar of time and space, but I'll take what I can get and breathe in every ounce of this magic at two miles a minute.

After hours of wonder, the coast again begins to draw closer from the right. It is almost a shame to bid this Martian landscape farewell and return to the more familiar coastal scenery. Like Port Hedland earlier in the day, a large white mass lies to the north of Carnarvon. It is Australia's western-most lake, Lake Macleod, and it also hosts several evaporative salt beds, but this time it is not the salt that catches my eye. On the hill beyond the airfield sits a huge white parabolic dish. It is an antenna of sizeable proportions and significant history.

'The Dish' at Carnarvon

Built in the 1960s, the satellite Earth Station at Carnarvon was called for to improve communications for NASA's moon landing project. In fact, the dish played a role in relaying Neil Armstrong's momentous first steps, live, to the Western Australian audience. However, time marches on and technology advances even more quickly. Now the dish sits dormant, yet dominating, on the Carnarvon hilltop.

Entering the circuit, the Gascoyne River lies below me, a dry river bed, impatiently waiting for the waters to return and flow into Shark Bay and onto the Indian Ocean. Even so, the banks are marked with green cultivated paddocks that have been absent over the last few hours of flight time. On the approach to land, I sight a row of Red Crosses parked on the hardstand. They are the tell-tale forms of six Air Force PC-9 trainers on exercise from RAAF Base Pearce near Perth. I return my eyes to the runway ahead, as there is a fair old wind blowing at Carnarvon and the convective turbulence is also playing its part in bouncing me around. Soon the rough ride is a memory and I am parked on the apron with the scarlet trainers on one side and a newspaper reporter on the other.

The interviews are becoming part of my daily routine, having undertaken around thirty in the past few days. I am busily answering questions when the refuelling truck pulls up beside the Jabiru and readies to fill its tanks for the final stage today. Being a Sunday, refuelling normally incurs a substantial additional fee for interrupting a peaceful day off. However, the gentlemen lowering the nozzle into the refuelling port will hear none of it as he is a staunch supporter of the Flying Doctor. I humbly appreciate his generosity but present him with a 'There and Back' baseball cap as a small token of thanks.

Royal Australian Air Force PC-9 trainers at Carnarvon

Set to go, one by one the PC-9s start their engines, so I delay my departure to take in the show. Like soldiers in formation, the line of turbo-prop trainers whistle past, perfectly paced and spaced. The smell of kerosene fills the warm air as they turn to enter the runway and position for takeoff, their sound subsiding as they move into the distance. Then, with rapid fire, they launch into the sky as if attached by a long invisible chord. Roaring past, they each snap into a brisk left turn at the same point above the runway, climbing overhead with enviable performance. And then they are gone, and the airfield is once again silent but for the wind and my lone voice calling "Clear Prop!" and bringing the Jabiru to life.

There is a little over an hour left in the air on my longest day of flying and yet the day is far from over. For despite the amazing day that I have witnessed from the air, it will be the hours after the aircraft has been put to rest that will impact me the most.

16

A SACRED SITE.

The graves of lost aviators

Day Five. Carnarvon – Kalbarri.

The final run home is 170 miles along the coast, beginning with the beautiful Shark Bay. With full tanks of fuel, sandy beaches below, and clear skies above, I decide to fly at least part of this last stage at the relatively low altitude of 500 feet above ground level. At 500 feet AGL, the detail in the scenery below becomes even more acute with individual trees and even leaves, easily discernible.

The world seems to pass by more quickly at this height and abandoned airstrips and dirt tracks come and go in a heart-beat. All the while the white sands are a constant companion out to my right-hand side with waves gently lapping the shore on isolated beaches. My mind has almost exceeded capacity absorbing the broad spectrum of colours and textures that I have seen today, and this coastal fringe provides even more. I want to yell the praises of this region to the world, but then pause, wondering if the key to its beauty lies in its isolation and sparse spattering of mankind.

Shark Bay in Western Australia

Almost on cue, the remnants of past habitation slip by beneath me, a ghost town. I wheel the Jabiru around and look down along the line of the wing, which seems to point at the structures below me. I guess it was once a thriving community of miners or farmers, now long gone. The buildings remain, blending back into the outback sands out of which they grew. Corrugated tin roofing flapping in the breeze and empty door frames open to the drifting sands, only the stone walls seem to offer any resistance to the onslaught of time and nature.

From above, they stand so alone and yet undoubtedly played host to hilarity, hope and heartache in grander times. All around the eye can see nothing but the horizon; still these pioneers staked their claim in this very spot. Now many undoubtedly lie in tiny graves on the small ridge a few miles up the road. I cannot help but wonder what stories these walls once told, now fallen silent and their words lost in time. The sound of my engine fades, too, as I level the wings and head south to Kalbarri.

The land ahead now begins to rise to meet me and I decide that is time to place some distance between the earth and me once again. As I track slightly inland, the beaches are gradually replaced by foliage and ridge lines, whose profile is becoming accentuated by the afternoon sun. I am now 'laying off' quite an amount of drift to counter the strong wind that is blowing, and I notice a discernible change in my speed across the ground. It has been a long day and my eyes are weary as I scan my chart to locate my lodgings for the night at Murchison Station. It lies on a bend in the river to the north of the airport, so I decide to follow the Murchison River that now looms large ahead.

Without difficulty I sight the few buildings that constitute the historic station and orbit overhead as requested to notify them of my arrival. Confident that I have made enough noise to attract their attention, I cut across to the airfield and descend into the circuit pattern. It soon becomes apparent that the breeze is also blowing at Kalbarri Airport, as the wind-sock seems to be almost at breaking point, although, thankfully, it is almost parallel in direction to the runway.

Approaching Kalbarri and Murchison Station

Even so, as I make the final turn to make my approach to land, there is a significant cross-wind component to this gusty wind. I am working very busily in the cockpit to control the Jabiru with my right hand on the yoke and doing my best to maintain some semblance of a constant approach speed and flight path with the throttle in my left. A gust rolls me without warning, and I quickly roll the wings back to level flight. It's an exciting ride and at times the speed washes off suddenly, leaving the Jabiru hanging in the air, void of energy, until I can offer her a dose of airspeed to carry on. All the while, I am very prepared to abandon the landing if it gets too hairy and I have enough fuel and daylight to fly to Geraldton, if need be. But for the moment, it is difficult, not dangerous.

The headwind means that it is a slow ride down to the runway where a Fokker 50 airliner is waiting to depart. I gather that I am the entertainment for the passengers and crew as they watch the mighty little Jabiru do battle with the conditions. Finally, the runway is within inches of the wheels and I ease in the rudder and lower one wing to align the aeroplane with the runway. Right in front of the critical audience of the Fokker's crew, I touch down, slow down and turn around. Phew!

My relief is echoed by the airliner's pilot who transmit "I'm glad that was you!" as they enter the runway and wait for me to get out of their way. I waste no time in doing so and as they roar into the sky, I swing the Jabiru into a small wind-break provided by some thick undergrowth and shut down the engine. I have been in the air for seven hours and fifty-five minutes of extraordinary flying, but now it's time to call it a day.

I climb out and push the Jabiru's tail well back toward the foliage before lashing her down very securely to a pair of concrete blocks. As I unload my gear, I share a few insights with a reporter from Kalbarri before my 'lift' arrives and I head off to Murchison Station for the night. The station owner, Calum, and his daughter sit in the front of the truck as I lean back on the seating in the rear in the company of a couple of fierce looking 'pig dogs'. Never a big fan of canines, these two dogs occasionally growl at each other as we bump along the dirt road, but thankfully seem disinterested in me.

The Fokker at Kalbarri patiently waits its turn.

Calum offers me an ice-cold beer and, although I have not consumed a single alcoholic drink on this trip so far, the frigid drops running down the side of the bottle are just too hard to resist at the conclusion of eight hours in the seat. As I drink the amber fluid, I can feel the cooling effect immediately and tip my head back in a thoroughly relaxed state, chatting with Calum as we drive on.

When we enter Murchison Station, there is a mix of buildings, the historic homestead, beautiful climbing plants, and even rusting military vehicles, including a tank. After nights in hotel rooms and cabins, the intimate surrounds of this historic, working station are just what I need. This station has been active for over one hundred and fifty years and I can't wait to stow my gear and absorb the history.

My historic room at Murchison Station

Calum shows me to my lodgings; they are refurbished shearer's quarters that were built by convicts in 1860. There are some tell-tale signs of their convict builders even today. The large door-bolt is only lockable from the outside, while the lone small window would not allow a man to escape. Inside, the walls have been rendered, but one small section has been framed and preserved to show its original form. The ceiling is low, but the air is cool by virtue of the thick stone walls. This is great!

As the sun is getting low, Calum suggests that we head straight out to the place that motivated me to stay at Murchison Station in the first place. I jumped back into a four-wheel drive and we trekked through the scrub until a small clearing emerged, spattered with headstones. A number of these headstones dated back to the founding days of the station, but it was two old headstones and a low fence that catch my eye.

Pausing beside the lost airmen

They are of Bob Fawcett and Eric Broad. They were contemporaries of Sir Charles Kingsford Smith and had been killed in 1921 when their Bristol Tourer biplane stalled while circling overhead a fellow aircraft that had been forced down with mechanical issues. The flight had been the first scheduled air service in Australia, a freight run, but was cut short in the wake of the tragedy. The outcome was that the service was placed on hold until sufficient emergency landing fields could be constructed throughout the Western Australian outback. During that time, QANTAS grew from strength to strength on the east coast, and the rest is history.

Now I stand at this remote, forgotten graveside, so significant to our aviation history and pay my respects to these lost aviators. As I do so, Calum points just over the way, for that is where the aircraft tragically struck the ground. The wind and the isolation only add to the solemnity of the site, and I am deeply moved.

I return to my shearer's quarters and sit on the verandah, chatting with some young transient backpackers who are working their keep at Murchison. Having a warm shower is like a shot in the arm and that night I share a meal with my hosts at the homestead and learn more of the history. It is a tremendous feast of chicken and vegetables that I consume at an embarrassing pace. Seated around a table on the lawn under the stars, stories change hands and Calum relates that when he first arrived that there were some ageing ladies who still recalled with a smile when 'Smithy' came to Murchison.

Once again, generosity comes to the fore and Calum and his wife Belinda insist that my night's stay is 'on the house' as their contribution to the work of the RFDS. Once again, I am embarrassed, grateful, and in admiration of the outback fellowship. We enjoy dessert and a couple more tales and the entire occasion feels more like old friends catching up than a host-guest-worker relationship. This is Australia at its egalitarian best.

The Murchison Station 'shearer's sheds'

I bid one and all goodnight and make my way by torchlight. There is no internet connection, so it is a night without news reports, interviews, blogs or updates. I stop to fill a jug of water in the kitchen, where a harmless python resides in the drawer, before walking to my room and unlatching the convict bolt to enter. My torch beam reveals a coating of huge moths on the corrugated ceiling, and I resolve to leave them alone if they'll reciprocate the favour. In minutes, I am horizontal and ready to sleep in the darkest room one can imagine; it's blissful.

I roll over to set the alarm on my phone and set some very soft music to play. I am totally relaxed. I can still hear the wind outside, and I think of my Dad and of the lost aviators' graves, miles from home. So much has happened since the sun rose in Broome. The music is still playing gently as I am lost to the world for the night.

17

BRIGHT LIGHTS. BIG CITY.

The Perth skyline comes alive.

Day Six. Kalbarri –Geraldton - Perth.

It's 3 a.m., and I'm woken gently by the murmurings of music still coming out of my phone beside the bed. I soon become aware that the sound that woke me is the thrashing of the wind that has increased in strength once again. I lie there, wondering whether I should abandon any further effort to sleep and just get underway. My heavy eyes decide otherwise, and I roll over, determined to sleep just a little longer.

Bang! Bang! Bang!

Right on time, Calum gives the old wooden door three loud raps and I bound out of bed with a yell of acknowledgement. As usual, my gear is ready to go and within minutes I'm in the truck, bounding down the track to the airport. The four-wheel drive's headlights peer into the darkness as the wheels bound from one pothole to another.

Kalbarri Airport seems eerily still as I toss my gear on the ground and shake Calum's hand. We wish each other luck and, moments later, his truck's red taillights disappear into the distance as he heads back to Murchison Station. The wind has again dissipated, and it is pitch black in every direction, with not even the moon to illuminate my surroundings. I reach into my bag and draw out a torch, whose beam subsequently pierces deep into the void.

I follow the beam across the tarmac to where the Jabiru sits silently. A shuffling in the scrub draws my attention and I have undoubtedly disturbed a nocturnal marsupial going about its duties. The shuffling ceases and now it is silent. Then, I turn off my torch and it is absolutely dark. A real sense of remoteness comes across me and I feel like I could be the only man on earth. My aircraft is only a few metres away, but it is invisible, lost in the all-consuming night.

Sitting on my kit bag, I remain still, depriving myself of all sensory input and allowing my mind to roam freely. It is the most relaxing feeling in the world and my thoughts wander to the aviators of old sleeping beneath their wings and the pioneer drovers at rest on their swags by the track. Removed from the digital drone and even human contact, I am at absolute peace and allow the silence to be broken only by drawing in the deepest of breaths before slowly expelling through my lips. I gradually raise my eyes to the sky and there are more stars than I have ever seen before. In the absence of city lights, nature's answer is a complex array of twinkling stars and steady planets tied together by a glowing mist reaching me through the passage of time.

This is one of the most peaceful moments of my life.

And then there is just an inkling; a slight hint of a glow. To my night-adjusted eyes, the distant light seems to be spreading rapidly and creating an edge between the night and the advancing day. About me, the undergrowth begins to emerge as shadowy forms from the darkness and the outline of the Jabiru seems to appear out of vapour. With each growing ray of light, my serenity is replaced by the spinning wheels within my brain. The pilot within is waking, elbowing my inner peace out of the way. "Enough ", it barks. "It's time to fly!"

The sun rises quickly as I load the last bags on board and begin my inspection of the trusty little two-seater. She is just as I left her the previous day, and I wonder how serene her night had been while I slept at Murchison. Minute by minute, the scenery gains an increasing level of detail and the stars have been replaced by full-blooded rays of sunlight as I slip on my sunglasses.

A memory etched in my mind forever: Sunrise at Kalbarri

I start the engine and then sit for some time, allowing the six cylinders beneath the cowling to warm their oil and come to pace with the new day. As the temperature gauges ease up from the amber toward the green, I organise my flight plans and paperwork, GPS, and radios. I check my watch and note the date is May 10th, my wedding anniversary. Kirrily and I knew that I would be away for our special day, but even so, it had crept up on me this week as I focussed intently on the flight. Thirteen years ago, I was readying to walk down the aisle. This morning I am readying to release the park brake. Again, I feel a little selfish for missing our anniversary as I wander the skies, but perhaps that's why my marriage is the best thing that I've ever done.

Kalbarri falls away, and I point the Jabiru's nose toward Geraldton and my only transit stop today. After two long days across the Kimberley and the Pilbara, I am grateful for a mere three and a half hours of flight time along the coast. For every inch further south that I trek, it seems that the grass becomes greener and more signs of civilisation emerge. Before long, a substantial township emerges with a small point of land extending to the sea and a welcoming airport and fuel tanker to the west.

As I pass overhead, I can see that the wind has returned to greet me and once again a substantial crosswind is on offer. With the choice of two runways, neither offers a landing into wind, so I opt for the longest runway and the shortest taxi to the terminal. By now, I am wondering what the Jabiru is like to land into a direct head-wind. As I cross the threshold, my ritual of rudder and roll combine to place one main-wheel and then the other onto the runway, before I lower the nose and slow the aircraft.

A few people are milling around the terminal, but on this occasion, they are not there for me, but the impending arrival of an airliner. I manoeuvre the Jabiru into a discreet parking space beside a shining red and white 'Piper Arrow' and shut down the engine. I have hardly turned off all the switches when the refuelling truck pulls up; keen to fill my tanks before the thirsty airliner arrives. I oblige by hopping straight out and loosening my fuel caps on top of the wings.

We chat as the cool Avgas pours into the tanks and I survey my surroundings. The terminal bears the name of Sir Norman Brearley, whose Bristol Tourers had flown into Murchison Station all those years ago. I cast an eye at the Piper Arrow next to me and admire the new paint that covers its skin and then I read the registration: VH-BME. It is one of the first aircraft that I learnt to fly.

Back then, it possessed chalky white paint with a blue and yellow stripe, not the glossy crimson it now displays. I sign for my fuel and then walk over to look at my old machine more closely. Its windows are now tinted and as I squint, I can see beautiful new upholstery inside. It has seemingly left its life of training and is now the pampered touring aircraft of a proud owner. My eyes hunt for familiar switches and dials amongst the additions that have been installed in the ensuing years.

Despite the differences, it was still within this airframe that I began to learn my trade twenty-five years and 16,000 hours of flight time ago. I sat there in that left-hand seat, and Dad sat beside me in the right. Together, we took to the skies and yet dad was not there for my most memorable flight. He waved me off on that occasion, but the flight was a long 'solo' cross-country exercise around country New South Wales.

My old bird 'Bravo Mike Echo' at Geraldton

It was not my first time navigating alone, but I vividly remember that it was the first time I had the opportunity to raise my head, content that all was in order and absolutely inhale the joy of flight. That day in BME so many years ago, I truly appreciated for the first time that an aeroplane was not merely a tortuous training device, but a means of transport offering freedom that I had never imagined. Now, all these years later, we are reunited, and I pat her flanks like a loyal old horse. And yet there is a slight wave of sadness, too, as this wonderful aeroplane is another reminder along the way that Dad is not here to share the moment. Although as the Jabiru's propeller turns over and I get underway once again, part of me feels like Dad is still there in the right-hand seat, casting a careful eye over proceedings.

Cruising along the coast, I have an urge to track down the owner of BME and buy the aeroplane. Such a sentimental plan stirs excitement within, but my practical voice once again wins the argument, and I am thankful to be sitting in a new Jabiru on another very long cross-country exercise. Jandakot Airport is the Perth's aerodrome for light aircraft. I have routinely flown into the capital city's major airport, but this is my first-time landing at Jandakot, so I ensure that I have all my charts at the ready as the wide-open airspace is replaced by the narrowing funnel of radar-control and 'lanes of entry'.

The coastal run to the north of Perth

There will be no wandering about the skies here, just precise, procedural navigation until I land. As always, I am conscious of the website transmitting my position to the world and the watching media, so I concentrate on not messing up.

To the north of Perth, the Air Force has a few training areas, so I have planned a route that avoids these areas before flying a coastal corridor to Jandakot. As my finger creeps across the chart and the aeroplane creeps down the GPS's screen, I am increasingly bounced about by turbulence. My eyes hunt between the map, the earth, and the instruments as I fight off the rough air's attempts to destroy my ability to focus.

I fly the 'lane' via Guilderton along the coast and hear several aircraft coming in the opposite direction. We use the radio to keep a safe distance from each other when the first Robinson helicopter passes below me, down the left-hand side. Now I excitedly await the passing of the next aircraft, and they are upon me within moments. A formation of scarlet Air Force trainers is off to the left of my nose and closing fast. PC-9 trainers like those I encountered at Port Hedland, although this group is far closer to home. In a heartbeat, they whistle past and their brightly coloured wings are set beautifully against the blue-green waters below.

Not long now. I follow the coast to the port at Freemantle and past the marinas and then cut inland to Jandakot. My eyes are now looking outside for other traffic as I navigate toward the airfield ahead as the city skyline passes to my left. I make my inbound radio call to Jandakot Tower and add the suffix, "unfamiliar with the airfield", to give them fair warning of the east-coast alien heading toward them.

Passing the marinas inbound to Jandakot.

Despite my fair warning and the anticipation of flying a full circuit pattern, the control tower tells me to sight and follow another aeroplane, make a straight-in approach to land and "keep the speed up." Now I have flown jets for years but keeping the little aerobatic aircraft ahead of me in sight and getting the Jabiru down from altitude without shock-cooling the engine kept this old pilot busy enough, thank you. With the runway ahead and ready to land, I could see the reason for the controller's haste; he had a long queue of aircraft were waiting to takeoff and he wanted me out of the way.

I made a respectable landing in front of the audience of other aeroplanes and cleared the runway, looking for the Royal Aero Club of Western Australia. The Jabiru would stay with the good folks of the RACWA and have a pre-arranged 'check-up' while I enjoyed a day off in Perth. The air traffic controller steered me in the right direction and a minute later, the modern clubhouse and long-established hangar were right in front of me.

Jandakot Arrival

I taxied onto the hard-stand near the aero club and adjacent to the maintenance facility. The Jabiru's engine fell silent as I deprived it of fuel and spark and this short day's flying was over. Radios off, lights are all off, switches are all off, etc. I double-check myself and my checklist. Finally, everything is in order, and I raise my head to look outside and almost fall out of the cockpit. There behind the fence, 2,000 miles from home is Kirrily. Happy Anniversary!

18

SOME REST AND RECREATION.

The Jabiru receives some attention.

Day Seven. Perth.

K irrily's surprise arrival had been perfectly timed. Today was not only our wedding anniversary, but tomorrow was a planned day of rest and recreation away from the flight. Her presence guaranteed that I would be able to switch off, wind down, and enjoy the day without probing or pondering some aspect of the remaining journey.

However, before we left Jandakot for our hotel, there was a visit to the RFDS Western Australian headquarters to attend. Receiving a very warm reception, we are shown around the base, including a close-up look at one of their Pilatus PC-12 aircraft. As I ponder the specialised medical interior, a ripple begins to stir through the base. An emergency call has been received, and one by one, my hosts politely excuse themselves and ready for departure.

The speed and efficiency that the team at the RFDS mobilise the Pilatus and its people is impressive. Without fuss or furore, everyone goes about their task and soon the familiar sound of the turbo-prop spooling up fills the air and the PC-12 is on its way. It is a very poignant reminder of the very people that this flight is seeking to support and reinforces the critical nature of their work.

Kirrily and I with an RFDS PC-12

Even as we leave the airport, we do so under the watchful gaze of a single-engined Mooney sitting atop a pole. This memorial recalls the selfless dedication of Robin Miller, a nurse, aviatrix and RFDS pilot. Fondly known as the 'Sugarbird Lady', she selflessly served the Aboriginal children of the outback in their battle against polio, flying great distances in her tiny aeroplane. Everywhere I look on this journey, there were reminders of the wonderful achievements of aviation in the name of humanity.

"Sugarbird Lady"

It is a thought that Kirrily and I discuss as we sit on the balcony of our hotel and watch the lights of the skyline grow increasingly brighter against the backdrop of the advancing night. Before it becomes too late, we make our way to a restaurant for an anniversary dinner and more conversation that threatened to continue late into the night. However, fatigue is holding the upper hand and I once again sleep deeply, not stirring until the daylight lit our room.

Opening the curtains, the Swan River is clearly visible. Home to the Australian leg of the Red Bull Air Race, it was here only weeks before that Adilson Kindlemann had put his aircraft into the water and where our own Matt Hall had stood on the podium in front of a home crowd. Many years before, nearby Langley Park had been the city's airfield, but now it was only the occasional home for the Red Bull racers as they took to the skies and ripped past the inflatable pylons.

Sitting here comfortably with a cup of tea in my hand seems almost alien. There is no pre-dawn ritual today and no equipment to lug down the road to the Jabiru. There is no flight plan to be submitted, although there are still media commitments. The setting for a leisurely day has been set and I don't need any encouragement to slip into the groove.

After lunch with my gorgeous wife, we meet her cousin Hayley and the family for a quick visit to the Jabiru. The whistle stop is partially to confirm that all the maintenance has been successfully completed, but mainly to allow the kids to crawl over the aircraft and pose for photos in the pilot's seat. Then it is off for an afternoon with family and a home-cooked meal that provides a shot of tonic both mentally and physically. By the time I lay my head down, I am relaxed yet ready to go once again.

My kit is packed, and the flight plan is submitted, so with a clear conscience and a comfortable bed I drift into another good night's slumber.

Kicking back in Perth

And despite a good eight hours of solid sleep, I already have one eye on the clock minutes before the alarm is set to sound. In the darkness, I switched the alarm setting to 'OFF' and slip into the bathroom for a shower and shave, endeavouring not to wake Kirrily. A short time later, the taxi's headlights are peering down the deserted city streets as we wind our way to the airport.

Family fun with the Jabiru

At Jandakot, the Royal Aero Club is well lit, but seemingly abandoned. With the Jabiru parked on the other side of the clubhouse, I scratch around looking for access but I'm unable to find any until a kindly cleaner lets us both in. Without further ado, the Jabiru is readied and loaded for the day ahead. It will be a day that sees me heading east for the first time on this flight and into the flat arid expanses of the Nullarbor Plain.

I have one final order of business to attend to: a radio interview with 2GB's Alan Jones. Amidst the cleaners' vacuums and hoses, I seek out a quiet corner to wait for the call from the Sydney-based talkback host. When the call comes, we chat about the centenary of flight and the flying doctor amongst a good many other subjects, including that my brother had worked on a book with Alan twenty years earlier. The 'Zupp' surname made that association inescapable.

The sun is now only just rising and already a good deal has been achieved. I bid Kirrily a warm farewell and a race challenge as she will soon to board an eastbound airliner. I figure that I could make it to Kalgoorlie just before she passes overhead in the stratosphere. We joked about that one more time and then I stir the well-rested Jabiru back to life. Without hesitation, she responds to my request and the shining wooden propeller bounces the sun's early rays back into my eyes. One more wave to my girl, a radio transmission, and then I release the brakes to get underway.

Departing Perth with the sun still low

A voice comes across the radio, and then another, all of them wishing me well. There wasn't another aircraft to be seen as I taxied out, but I gather they, too, were not far away from taking to the skies. Kirrily was still there, filming, as I line up on the runway, pointing into the sun. Squinting through my sunglasses, I ease the throttle forward and the Jabiru's wheels begin to turn on the asphalt. Gathering speed, the aeroplane smells the air and nudges me through the control column to set her free.

I respond by easing back on the stick, although the Jabiru needs very little encouragement. The airflow rushes over the wings and the crisp, clear morning air envelopes the fuselage. These are the mornings to fly. There is a frontal system moving in behind me, but I estimate having a couple of day's head start on that wind and rain. Now I am heading east and pointing homeward with half of the miles behind me. Yet there is quite a way and a good many amazing moments still to go.

19

FINDING FORREST.

Day Eight. Perth - Kalgoorlie - Forrest.

I check my watch and figure that Kirrily will be at Perth Airport by now and boarding her jet very soon. Ahead of me, the sun's glare is a constant reminder of my eastward track and serves as both a God-send and a nuisance. I squeeze my way from Jandakot through the thin corridor of air trapped between the rising ground and the invisible bounds of the congested controlled airspace above me.

Gradually, the hills give way to plains and the houses to homesteads. As I push further inland, the beautiful sense of space that had characterised the first half of the flight begins to return as the coastal fringe fades behind me. For all the majesty of the shoreline, there is something about the wide-open spaces that connects deeply with my soul. A sense of freedom that can only come with isolation and is best enjoyed from my vantage point aloft. The engine hums and I smile as one patchwork acre after another lies out before me.

Paddocks to the east of Perth

My map is pinned beneath my thigh and I check the vital elements of fuel and time off on my flight plan before reaching across and retrieving a Muesli Bar from the depths of my backpack. Small airfields can be seen from time to time. Some are farmer's strips, while others appear to host gliders or those hardy souls that leap from aeroplanes. Either way, I make a mental note of their whereabouts and the safe haven they offer.

Divots begin to appear in the turf below and the flatlands boast contours. The land is changing in its character. Some is by the hand of nature, while the white pock-marks are evidence of man scratching the surface in search of something deeper. The mines become increasingly frequent, as do the roads that weave between them. Kalgoorlie now lies only half an hour ahead and its rooftops are beginning to glint in the sun.

For more than a century, Kalgoorlie has harvested gold from the earth and today the 'Super Pit' dominates its geography. This huge, open cut, diamond mine is two miles long and a mile wide and works around the clock. The huge single pit has replaced the series of underground mines where multitudes of miners had toiled for decades. As I manoeuvre the Jabiru to land, the sheer enormity of this massive hole in the ground is daunting. Just as the Argyle diamond mine had sheared off the end of a mountain range, this 'Super Pit' has gouged down deeply into the bowels of the earth.

The squeaking of the Jabiru's wheels touching down reminds me of my life on a far smaller scale and I taxi to the fuel bowser to fill the tanks once more. At first, my refuelling efforts are foiled by a series of error codes and an absence of flowing fuel. I look about longingly for a smiling face and a tanker, but neither can be seen, so I continue to swipe my card and punch in the numbers. Finally, I discover a concealed 'reset' button and the digits on the bowser come to life signalling that it is time to climb the ladder and quench the Jabiru's thirst.

The Kalgoorlie "Super Pit"

The temperature of the metal nozzle in my hand drops noticeably as the fuel flows through and the tell-tale vapours begin to escape from the rim around the fuel cap. There is a strange sense of satisfaction in the act that reminds me of leading a loyal horse to an oasis after a long ride. It is a sentiment that is lost on this lifeless blend of metal and composite materials and yet it has been no less loyal.

Beside me, an old Royal Flying Doctor's hangar still carries the markings from many years past and a little beyond it is a museum dedicated to the RFDS. Every fuel stop is different. Some are brief and isolated, while others are longer with people to meet and sights to see.

At Kalgoorlie, there is a phone interview with the lads from Plane Crazy Down Under and some wonderful folks that have come by the airport to say hello. The Flying Doctor staff show me through their museum and give me a free teddy bear to keep my mascot, Bert, company on the flight ahead. The warmth of the country folk is the same across the breadth of the nation. Honest, hard-working people that love the land that surrounds them. I love it, too.

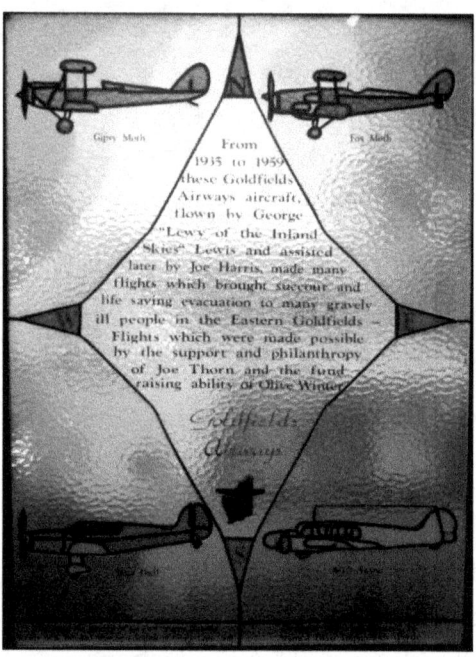

A stained-glass window in the RFDS gallery at Kalgoorlie

Reluctantly, Kalgoorlie has only been a whistlestop and it's time to climb back on board and set course. As I climb away and raise the flaps, the cavernous pit once again captures my attention and I wheel about its perimeter at a respectful distance, looking down into its deep heart. From here, I level the wings and ready myself for a remote, but relaxing, three and a half hours to Forrest and just shy of the South Australian border.

Gun-Barrel Straight

Through this landscape's heart runs a silver needle that joins the nation from east to west. It is a gun-barrel straight rail-line that has been the life-blood across the Nullarbor Plain for nearly one hundred years. Nullarbor hails from the Latin meaning "no trees" and it is a reasonably apt name for the remote miles that lie ahead. Below me, the land has become billiard table flat and taken on a rich, rusty red colour. Trees are few and far between, and scrub and Spinifex are the only noticeable vegetation.

Yet the absence of features to navigate by does not pose a problem, for I have an aid even more reliable than a GPS: that gun-barrel railway. At regular intervals, it boasts a railway siding or a dirt airstrip where the RFDS can land. Occasionally a quarry or a bore passes by, but really there is very little else. Mile after mile ticks by and Kasey Chambers' 'Nullarbor Song' softly rolls through my mind. If that silver line stays just outside my window, I will hit Forrest and I relax in that thought.

This reassurance allows me to relax and reflect about this wonderful flight. In my mind's eye, I look down upon the Jabiru again, a small white speck crossing this vast red expanse. This anonymity and isolation is such a far cry from the radio chatter and rigid flightpaths of airline flying. If I wish to go to the left, there is no need for an airway's clearance and I simply nudge the stick a little to the side. If I wish to circle about and take a closer look at the ruins of a building, I am able to do so. This is flight. This is freedom.

And if I desire to say hello to the train ahead, then the choice is mine. So, I lower the nose and take the Jabiru down slowly and gently, parallel to the railway line. The train's form is the only break in the consistent shining silver of the tracks, and gradually I draw closer, bringing the Jabiru into level flight at just 500 feet above the desert soil. I come alongside the train and lazily rock the wings to say "G'day", imagining that there may be a child with their nose pressed against the train's window and waving back.

A train crossing the Nullarbor

As I pass the motor at the front, I am sure that the driver must be watching, so I slow down for a moment with my flaps extended to offer a better view. The two of us are heading east at a rate of knots, but there is little else to be seen here. I accelerate and draw ahead, climbing back up to altitude for the home stretch to Forrest. I wonder when the train will make it to the distant coast and how far ahead will I be by the day's end? One more waggle of my wings and then I resume my routine. Fuel is good. Time is good. And the silver line still sits by my window.

Finally, my oasis appears ahead, a small cluster of buildings and a runway so black that I wonder how old the asphalt is. As I turn overhead, it is obvious that it has been recently resurfaced as the centreline and piano keys are a brilliant white. I am miles from anywhere and this is the 'cleanest' runway I have ever seen. As I line up on my final approach to land, my shadow sits out to my right, skipping across the scrub. My video camera is pointing in the general direction, capturing the image of the closing shadow.

Forrest from above

The runway now sweeps beneath my wheels and my shadow merges with its owner. More than six hours of flying have passed, but each minute was magical, caught between the red earth and the clear blue skies. The caretaker of this airside 'truck stop' welcomes me and we chat about the Jabiru as I ready her for bed. He helps me push the replenished little aeroplane into the far corner of a very large and very old hangar where it is kept company by the battered wreck of an old Cessna 206. Along with a guest house, this vintage hangar had once provided overnight accommodation for weary West Australian Airways passengers as they crossed the continent in the 1930s.

We drive back to my accommodation where I'll check in for the night and organise what time we will all sit down for a home-cooked dinner. As we rumble along the road, my mobile phone buzzes and beeps with a string of messages whose common theme is one of concern for my well-being. Intrigued, I make some phone calls and a couple of events have transpired since I left Kalgoorlie. Firstly, it seems as though my 'train waving' has caused concern for those watching my Spidertracks position plots on the internet. A number of followers had watched my slow, gentle descent down to 500 feet and wondered whether I had fallen asleep as I crossed the Nullarbor! I quickly set about reassuring everyone that rather than a source of concern, that short segment of flight in the lower levels was a highlight and I was very much awake throughout.

More seriously, as I was safely above the Nullarbor, a news story was breaking of a serious air crash at Jandakot Airport. Several messages are confirming that I am not the unfortunate aircraft involved, and again I seek to reassure the callers. Still, the thought is a sobering reminder of the potential dangers that flight can present and I recall the faces of friends that have died doing what they love. I also wonder if the crew of the ill-fated aeroplane was one of those that wished me well as I departed Perth earlier that day. I hope they are all OK.

The vehicle comes to a halt and I am stirred from my thoughts. My accommodation is one of the long-established cabins that I am told once housed meteorological bureau staff. The guest book is filled with names including those of the RAAF Aerobatic team, the Roulettes, and a good friend's wife. My father had paused in Forrest in 1955 when he deployed with a squadron of jet fighters for a military exercise in Perth. I have a photo of his Gloster Meteor parked here and I recall how he described the take off as the fuel-laden British jet struggled in the oppressive Australian heat.

Once again, I feel like Dad is just over my shoulder and I wonder if he had stayed in this very cabin where I am to sleep. It is a thought that I entertain as I walk through my lodgings and check out each and every room. Could he have been here? A chill runs up my spine and instantly I feel very close to Dad again, even though he has been gone for so long. His presence motivates me not to reflect further, but to sit down and organise my charts for the day ahead. That's what he would've done.

I speak with family, my support crew, and the media before I make my way to the homestead for dinner. A sumptuous meal of steak and vegetables is served up and it is just what I needed. Seeing that I have inhaled the food, my hosts offer me more. I decline with a level of embarrassment, and then they explain that it will go to waste.

The old 'West Australian Airways' hangar at Forrest

It transpires that some other pilots had also booked accommodation for the night and then not arrived. No notice. No phone call. With the nearest shop hundreds of miles away, my hosts had defrosted enough food for the anticipated number of guests and now it was set to be wasted. I enjoyed the additional offerings but quietly cursed the rudeness of my fellow aviators' thoughtlessness in these days of mobile phones and the internet.

We all chat for hours and they warn of the racket created through the night as the trains barrel through Forrest. I tell them of my journey and they explain how they had come to be the caretakers of this remote, historic wayside stop. Looking at the time, I excuse myself and wander in the dark back to my cabin. A chill has fallen, so I attempt repeatedly to start the gas heater without success. On my last attempt, I manage to initiate ignition, but obviously some gas was loitering in the area from my previous attempts. Bang!

My home for the night. Is this where my Dad once slept?

The noise punches my ears and the flash almost blinds me as I am sat fairly on my backside. I curse my own stupidity as I close off all the valves and open the windows to clear the air. I give up on the heater and climb into my comfortable old-style bed in a room filled with old-style furniture. I read a few pages of a book by the bedside lamp before I flick the switch and settle down in the darkness. I drift off within minutes and I never hear the racket of those midnight trains.

20

HEADING SOUTH.

A cliff face along the Great Australian Bight

Day Nine. Forrest-Ceduna-Port Lincoln.

When I do wake, there is absolute silence. The sun is low, and a light breeze is struggling to move the leaves on the trees outside my window. Sitting on the verandah, my eyes are free to wander far beyond the limits of my eyesight toward the very distant horizon. A still and calm surrounds me to such a degree that I can breathe it deeply into my lungs and feel the relaxation spread through my being. It is a sense that is impossible to grasp amidst the hustle and bustle of cities and suburbia.

I make a cup of tea and breakfast and take a moment to gather my thoughts. With my gear at the ready near the screen door, there's no particular hurry today, even though I am still technically in Western Australia, 'losing' an hour and a half when I cross the border. There is only a little over three hours flying to complete today and the sky above me is as clear as a bell. I just need to fly south to the coast and turn left and even I should be able to manage that without too much stress.

I field my morning call from ABC Radio as I wander from my lodgings across to the hangar where the Jabiru has spent the night. I wheel her out and load her up in a routine that has become second nature and progressively more efficient as the journey has progressed. Soon the still calm air is rushing over my wings and I am back in the skies, bidding Forrest farewell.

South of Forrest the red earth continues, with only Eucla Airfield interrupting the scrub's sparse covering. The airport consists of little more than multiple criss-crossing scratches in the dirt that constitutes the runways. I had originally entertained the idea of camping there for the night before opting for a solid roof over my head at Forrest. As I fly overhead, I suspect that I had made the right decision.

Now the coast is close, and the scrub gives way to the dramatic drop of vertical cliffs. I fly past at right angles to enhance the sense of launching from the cliffs and soar out over the waters of the Great Australian Bight before turning back toward the nation's southern edge. Once again, I am captivated by the diversity and contradictions of Australia's landscape. At times, the scenery is endless and repetitive, although not monotonous to my admiring eyes. Then there are instances where a reversal of landscape can occur in a matter of a few miles. And this is one such occasion.

As I look back at the land mass, I can see the dead, flat expanse extending toward Forrest, but only a few miles south of Eucla it gives way to brilliant aqua waters and crashing waves. The cliff faces are a dramatic cross-section of time, like someone has sliced through a layered cake. Two hundred feet high, the layers of different coloured limestone are topped by shallow soil with massive rock piles at the base. The waters are shallow, but incredibly clear, and I glimpse a shark swimming beneath me, prompting me to fly a little closer to the shore.

I settle in to fly parallel to the coast and the highway, observing the occasional truck or Grey Nomads with a trailer in tow. Still, it is the geology that fascinates me. The stark white limestone band that runs steadily along the cliff face like a cream filling is occasionally interrupted by stripes of red running down through the layers. At the 'Head of the Bight', the cliffs give way to expansive beaches and sandy plains, and once again there is the temptation to land at drink in the isolation. But onward I fly.

Ceduna is just around the corner and soon I am overhead, looking down on a windsock that is blowing so hard it is threatening to rupture. The conditions make for an exciting approach to land as the Jabiru is buffeted about in the turbulence, and a strong crosswind is on offer again regardless of which runway is used.

The Great Australian Bight, layered limestone, and a lone shark

I control the 'Jab' but allow it to ride out the worst of the bumps; there's no point in fighting it too aggressively. Eventually, the runway passes beneath and I squeeze in the rudder to line up with the centreline and lower the wing to avoid being blown downwind. The gusts are strong, and I still have a trickle of power applied as the first wheel eases onto the runway. Soon, the other two follow suit and I slow the aircraft to a crawl in the lumpy air.

Once again, I seem to be the only person at the airport as I refuel the Jabiru. A truck blasts by on the highway and toots his horn and soon after a couple of 'easy riders' on their Harley Davidsons do the same. Then they are gone, and the wind is the only constant presence that remains.

The Ceduna Airport Passenger Terminal

I do battle with the crosswind one more time and set out for Port Lincoln on the southern tip of the Eyre Peninsula. I climb above the turbulence, but the wind is ever present as the colours below begin to change once again. Patchy scrub and sandy plains are now being replaced by genuine vegetation and the first signs of agricultural activity. A host of blues and greens emanate from the beautiful waters of Streaky Bay and sand bars push up toward the surface.

The cliff faces, too, have transformed. Rather than towering, jagged edges they are smaller and subtler, rounded at their tops by erosion and the constant winds, I suspect.

Streaky Bay

I continue south along the coastline before turning to the east to cross the peninsula over farmlands and hamlets of habitation. For the first time since the Western Australian coast, hills begin to appear, and the landscape develops a series of rolling undulations.

The wind is still fierce when I arrive at Port Lincoln, although it is blowing straight down the runway. Consequently, my landing flare closely resembles the act of hovering as I am so very slow over the ground when the wheels finally touch down on the runway. Taxiing in to refuel and park, I am struck by the number of Cessna 337s around the airfield in various states of serviceability. These aircraft are novel in that they have one propeller at the front and one at the rear in a 'push-pull' arrangement.

The Eyre Peninsula's west coast

My Kununurra Cessna 337 back in the 1980s

The military version was immortalised in the movie *Bat 21* about a Forward Air Controller in Vietnam, but the aircraft met with limited success in civilian life. I had flown one in the Kimberleys many years before, but today they are still popular on Port Lincoln in the fish-spotting role in this 'Tuna Town'. Everywhere I look, I see these old birds.

I tie the Jabiru down with an extra level of security given the gale that is present. As I tie the final knot, a reporter from the local newspaper comes by for a chat and we speak equally about the flight and our common love of the game of cricket. It is a refreshing off-topic conversation that continued as he drove me to my caravan park for the night.

I bid him farewell and meet with the warmest of welcomes from the caravan park staff who show me to my lodgings. The caravan is clean and cosy and reminds me of my accommodation as a young charter pilot in Kununurra. I have hardly unpacked when I realise that I have left the GPS in the aircraft. Grrrr... For the first time, my flight-planning routine will have to take on a new look, leaving me to enter the route into the GPS the next morning. As a creature of habit, I don't particularly like doing this, but it's not a major hurdle.

There is a knock at the door and another warm welcome from the Lions Club and RFDS Auxiliary people. I am whisked away to a lovely barbeque where I am shown the fantastic work these community groups undertake to support the Flying Doctor. To a backdrop of cold drinks and sizzling sausages, I make a short speech about my journey thus far and some of the many highlights.

Port Lincoln, South Australia

Still more funds are raised for the RFDS and the tally continues to grow toward my goal of $10,000. Day after day, I am impressed and endeared by the honest nature of the people and communities that I encounter away from the hustle and bustle of the big city lights. All too soon the evening is over, and I am back in my caravan to flight-plan and settle in for the night.

Outside, the wind is blowing with violence and the temperature is dropping by the minute. I am thankful that I had taken the time to secure the Jabiru properly but curse myself again for leaving the GPS in the aeroplane. With nothing left to do, I settle in for the night to the accompaniment of the howling winds and my creaking walls.

The next morning the wind is still fierce as I sit in the comfort of a cafe eating a hot bacon and egg roll while the windows shudder. As I chow down, I survey the map of Australia that is posted on the wall nearby. I mentally track around the edges where I have travelled and contemplate the miles that are still to come. My eyes loiter on the piece of NSW that is home and I think of my kids beginning to stir and ready themselves for the day ahead. And that is what I now need to do as well.

I haul my gear back to the caravan park office to settle my bill and get underway. To my total surprise, the wonderful staff refused to take my money, winking that the owner lives interstate anyway. They emphasise that everyone in this town is so appreciative of the work of the Flying Doctor and if I am helping the RFDS, then they want to help me. I am touched by their generosity and thank them with more than a hint of embarrassment.

At the airport, the Jabiru was jiggling on its ropes and waiting for me. I leave her tied down as I load my gear and finally program the GPS for the day's flight to Adelaide via a rather indirect but historic route. I had originally planned for this day to visit Woomera, the home of Australia's space program in the 1950s and 60s; It is still a test range for military weapons, technology, and tactics. Despite obtaining the correct clearances well in advance, they were withdrawn when it became apparent that the Japanese space probe Hayabusa was due to crash on the Woomera range. It was a disappointing amendment to my flight plan, but there was still a lot to achieve here in South Australia.

This is my first leg over water, so I pull on my bulbous Air Force issue 'flotation jacket' and life vest. I place my emergency beacon in my pocket and attach the strap to my belt to avoid it coming loose in the event of a hurried evacuation. Rugged-up and ready to go, there is nothing left to do but fly, so I unlash the aircraft and stir it into life. The engine slowly warms up and I patiently wait to see all of my engine instruments nestled nicely in their respective 'green bands'. Satisfied that both man and machine are ready for flight, I complete the last of the engine-runs and checks before lining up on the runway.

The wind is on the nose of the aircraft as I accelerate down the runway. I quickly have enough air over the wings to fly and the Jabiru takes to the sky, climbing at a very impressive angle over the earth by virtue of the substantial headwind. I am underway for another day, but not ready to leave Port Lincoln just yet.

21

HISTORY, HEROES AND HEARTFELT THANKS.

Harry Butler's Bristol M1C

Day Ten. Port Lincoln-Minlaton-Adelaide.

The Spencer Gulf is known for its hungry population of Great White sharks. Having seen a sleek form slipping through the waters of the Great Australian Bight yesterday, I am determined not to become bait. To minimise the risk and maximise my gliding range, I climb steadily overhead the safety of Port Lincoln's runways to gain valuable altitude. As I do so, it gives the engine every opportunity to settle into its rhythm and offer me a little more time to confirm that all is in order.

Levelling off at a 'non-standard' 6,500 feet, I know that my altitude will give me around ten miles of gliding range in still air. Consequently, if I island-hop across the Gulf, I will be very close to making land even if the engine should fail at the most critical time. The bare mathematics makes me feel warm inside, so contentedly I set course to the south east and track toward Thistle Island with Cape Catastrophe sitting out to my right.

All is well with the world as I continue on this short overwater leg. The calm waters are bouncing the light of the brilliant morning sun up into my cockpit creating glare from above and below. Wedge Island passes by and the Yorke Peninsula now sits about thirty miles ahead. Not too far away sits Kangaroo Island and if time was not of the essence I would be sorely tempted again to turn right and make an unscheduled on Australia's third largest island.

Wedge Island in the Spencer Gulf

Inhabited for thousands of years by Aboriginals, it became more known for a good many shipwrecks in the years of European settlement. Today it is known for tourism as visitors from around the world take in its raw beauty and wildlife. I feel a strong urge to be a tourist, too, but the coastline ahead and the township of Minlaton beckons.

Sitting in the middle of the peninsula, Minlaton boasts a population of around 800 people and an aviation pedigree of the highest order. This small town was home to Captain Henry John 'Harry' Butler AFC, a World War One pilot and winner of the Air Force Cross. Returning from the war in 1919, Butler brought with him two Army surplus aeroplanes in the hope of kick-starting aviation in his native region. His return was accompanied with all manner of flights and barnstorming, but the one that made history was his flight across the Spencer Gulf with a couple of bags of mail from Adelaide. Alone in his tiny scarlet Bristol M1C monoplane, Butler wore an inflated tyre tube as a life preserver for the crossing that saw thousands turn out to meet him.

Below me I can see a couple of cars waiting for my arrival as I turn about the sky and bring the Jabiru back to earth. One of those meeting me is the great-nephew of Harry Butler and we strike up a great conversation in an instant. As we enter the town it is evident that Harry Butler is gone, but most definitely not forgotten. A large mural of him in uniform adorns a wall in the main street but even more significantly, his little red Bristol still resides in a purpose-built enclosure.

Inside, a stepladder is positioned for me to take a closer look, but first I circle the aircraft slowly, taking in its finer details. The polished, wooden propeller and the rich, red fabric stretched taut over the fuselage's framework, finished with a large Air Force roundel of red, white, and blue. The wings are braced by a series of wires that come together at the apex of a pyramid framework that sits atop the lone cockpit, and I imagine that climbing on board was not an easy task for the pilot. This is flight at its primitive best, and I am in awe of both man and machine in equal measures.

When I do ascend the ladder and stare down into the cockpit, my mind drifts even further back into time. A few basic dials are mounted on a wooden panel down the right-hand side to indicate altitude, airspeed, RPM, and little else. Thin control cables run along each side of the metal seat from their anchor points on the control column and rudder pedals. But even more moving than the simplicity of this workspace is the light film of dust that coats it. It is as if Harry has just climbed out of the cockpit and left the Bristol frozen in time.

I reach down and touch the control column, and I immediately feel connected. I can see his gloved hands, the goggles on his face, the inflated tyre tube, and a mailbag stuffed into the small remaining space. The smells drifting back from the tiny Le Rhone engine and the deafening noise drilling into the ear canals. Butler was a pioneer, and I can only wonder what he would make of today's monolithic Airbus A380s or even my extremely efficient Jabiru. So much has changed in a century.

The Bristol Cockpit

The little Bristol is left behind, and I am taken to the town's museum where more of Butler's belongings are to be found amongst other mementos of a country down that has served its nation in war and peace. The small rooms are packed with pieces of history and my head is spinning, trying to digest all that is on display and the tales behind the artefacts. Minlaton is a very small town with a very proud history.

Next. we gather for a bite of lunch and I cannot help but order the local fare of Spencer Gulf Garfish; I am not at all disappointed. It is as fresh as any fish I've tasted, and I inquire about the fishing industry from the locals that are seated about me. However, they seem more interested in the Jabiru and the fact that I had just transited the Gulf in a single-engined aeroplane. A burly-looking fisherman smiles at me through gritted teeth, half shaking his head before asking me, "Do you know how many bloody sharks are out there?" It causes a ripple of laughter from one and all as I acknowledge that uncomfortable fact.

A ballad about Harry Butler is performed and a wine cooler is passed around for donations to the RFDS. I gratefully accept the donation on behalf of the Flying Doctor and field some more questions about the flight so far. I could stay with these good people and good food a good while longer, but the bulk of the day's flying still lies ahead. Reluctantly, we make tracks once again, but the drive back to the airfield provides one more sight to see on the way. We pull over to the side of the road where a small memorial is placed near an open field.

I read the plaque which describes this site as the place where Harry Butler crashed an Avro biplane on the 11th January 1922. He was badly injured in the accident and died suddenly of a cerebral abscess in 1924 at the age of 34. The inscription reads that "this crash led to his death". It is a very sobering moment for me. Throughout my visit, Harry has deservedly been hailed as a hero, yet here in this unremarkable paddock, a remarkable man's dreams effectively came to an end. I am reminded of all that have made the supreme sacrifice in the advance of aviation and feel a pang of guilt in possessing the simplicity and safety that I enjoy in this modern day. Rest in peace, Harry.

Harry Butler's Memorial

The feeling stays with me as I climb away over fenced pastures and the occasional rising pall of smoke as farmers 'burn off' in the coolest time of the year. The saline expanse of Lake Gilles is ahead and cues me to start tracking eastward away from the Yorke Peninsula. All the while my engine ticks over sweetly, the GPS map scrolls, and the Spidertracks system broadcasts my position across the internet. What would Harry think?

My history lesson is still incomplete as I set heading for the boyhood home of one of Australia's greatest heroes. And yet many Australians do not even know his name. Try this on for size. The youngest of thirteen children, he joined the Australian Flying Corps in 1917 before transferring to another branch and serving as an official war photographer. In this role as a correspondent, he was thrown into the heart of the war and was awarded not one, but two Military Crosses for his heroic actions.

After the war he served as an ornithologist on the 'Quest' alongside

Ernest Shackleton and subsequently planned his own expedition to the North Pole in a submarine. He got within a few hundred miles before his hopes were dashed, but later in life, he would pioneer flight in the arctic regions. Oh, and by the way, he would sell one of his old aircraft to a bloke named Kingsford Smith who renamed it the 'Southern Cross'. He was knighted and in death, his ashes were scattered at the North Pole by the crew of a US naval submarine. All this in a single life, and although he is revered in the United States, he is almost overlooked by his native Australia. He was Sir Hubert Wilkins, another of my boyhood heroes alongside Bert Hinkler.

His childhood homestead sits one hundred miles to the north of Adelaide, but the diversion from my ultimate destination is well worth the effort. His home lies in a band of territory where drought can strike hard, and it was this harsh weather that led to Wilkins' lifelong interest in climatology. After I pass the township of Hallett, his sandstone cottage comes into view. Set back from the road a little, it is both sturdy looking and isolated. A new steel roof shines in the sun and is evidence of the extensive restoration work that was inspired by Dick Smith back in 1993.

Knights of the Air: Charles Kingsford Smith with Hubert Wilkins (right)

The homestead sits off my wingtip, and I marvel at how this great man came from such a humble beginning. His remarkable story should fill schoolbooks, but instead, even educated folks scratch their head at the mention of his name. I want to reach out and touch the sandstone and walk about the paddock, but this is as close as I can get as the Jabiru waltzes overhead lazily. I roll the wings level and take one last look before I head south to the capital city of Adelaide and all that goes with city life. I resolve to make the pilgrimage one day, but for the moment that lone dwelling begins to recede in the miles behind me.

The harsh terrain of Sir Hubert Wilkins' childhood

After days of silent radios and open skies, the red lines on my charts and the chatter in my headsets remind me that I am closing in on congested airspace. I follow the coastline north of Adelaide to transit the Outer Harbour on the way to Parafield Airport. I entertain the thought that it should be called Wilkins Field, or something similar, and a wry smile creeps across my face. My day has been filled with emotional moments and close encounters with great aviators. A good proportion of me just wants to pause and reflect, but now is not the time. Now is the time to follow that Grob trainer in my twelve o'clock and ensure that I land on the correct one of Parafield's many runways.

Lined up to land, I observe an unusual sight near the airfield fence. It appears to be a Gloster Meteor jet of the type that my father flew during the Korean War. A rarity in this day and age, it is sitting forlornly exposed to the elements with little more than a canvas cover to protect its canopy. The sad sight passes by me as I raise the nose and land the Jabiru a short distance away. As I taxi in and park,

I look across and notice the markings "A77-867" on the silver jet's flanks, and I scribble it down on the corner of my flight plan.

A Gloster Meteor F8 fighter jet

I am met by Bas Scheffers, who would go onto be one of the men behind the OzRunway's iPad app. Bas kindly gives me a lift to my accommodation and offers to escort me on my departure the next morning, which I gratefully accept. In the meantime, I check in at Flight Training Adelaide, or FTA, where I have kindly been provided with a room amongst their student pilot lodgings. I am given a guided tour of the base and cannot help but be impressed by the modern facilities. We enter the main building where all is in readiness for a course graduation dinner that night, to which I have been invited.

I had previously accepted another dinner invitation with my wife's cousin Raelene and her family which I was looking forward to but promised that I would drop by the function on my return. Dinner with family was what I needed more at that time as I needed to switch off from the flight for just a little while and Raelene's change of scenery provided that. I am missing my own wife and kids, so to share a table in a family setting is just what the doctor ordered, and we all laugh well into the evening.

By the time I arrive back at Parafield, the last student is being carried out the main doors on somebody's shoulders, so I gather that the official formalities are over. I envy their youth and the fact that their career is still ahead of them, but I don't envy how tired they will feel in the morning as I will be stirring well before the sun rises.

I shower and call home before I retire for the night. It is good to hear Kirrily's voice and I share with her the significance of the heroes and the history that I had encountered in the day's travels. I also tell her of the Meteor 867 on the airfield perimeter and how it always seems that Dad was never far away. The line went quiet and then I can hear the flicking of pages. It is Kirrily looking through one of my father's log books on my desk at home. Kirrily needn't have said it, but she did, "Your Dad flew 867."

22

ACROSS BASS STRAIT.

Day Eleven. Adelaide-Hamilton-Launceston.

My sleep is deep, but images of old aviators creep into my mind, speaking to me in muffled tones through Gosport Tubes and leather helmets. Their voices grow louder and begin crackling and stir me from my sleep. The clock reads 2:51 a.m. and far from the voices of Wilkins and Butler, they are the dulcet tones of a security guard outside my window chatting to his mate. Ugh. I have to get up in a couple of hours. Fortunately, I manage to eke out more precious sleep until the alarm startles me awake.

The weather forecast for today's flying is once again outstanding. There may be some fog patches, but these should clear to a brilliant day. Launceston is my destination, so there is a crossing of Bass

Strait to Australia's island state of Tasmania. The 150-mile stretch of water is broken midway by King Island, which is famous for its 'Double Thick Cream' and all manner of produce. Based upon the predicted weather, I should have an unbridled view of its green pastures as I fly overhead. I'm set to go.

An early start in Adelaide

Bas is preparing his aircraft in a distant hangar by the time I arrive at the Jabiru. The morning is brisk; small puffs of fog form on my breath, and a thin speckling of ice sits on the wings' leading edges. I carefully wipe the ice away and check the rest of the airframe for lurking sheets of ice. The phone rings and it's ABC radio calling for their daily update. Their support has been tremendous throughout the flight, but as I answer a range of questions this time, I find myself distracted by the first glow of dawn illuminating the horizon. It is stunning and silently grows in its majesty behind the outline of the Jabiru. I take the time to sit down on my kit-bag and watch the day's arrival, for these are the moments to hold on to.

Finally, I stir into action and Bas and I make our way toward the runway. We depart as a loose gaggle rather than a formation, although the sight of another aeroplane beside me is novel after thousands of miles of solitude. We track past a power sub-station and over the hills, and soon it is time for Bas to head back to Parafield. With a wave of his wings, he is gone; I settle into my routine for the six hours of flying that lies ahead.

The Murray River comes and goes, and I marvel at the detail I can see from this altitude. Six times each week, I pass overhead at 300 knots and umpteen thousand feet, but I can rarely truly see what lies below, perhaps a snaking river and a gathering of buildings here and there, but not much more. Down low, I can see cars going about their business and individual livestock in the pastures. Poles and power-lines, footpaths, and swimming pools all combine to make a detailed tapestry of the town below. Flying is such a privilege.

Not far beyond the Murray, the occasional fog patches are joining up to become an extensive blanket. My first fuel stop is Hamilton in Victoria, but theoretically I have enough fuel to fly to Launceston non-stop. However, a diversion to Melbourne or back to Adelaide would be a more likely scenario. Eerily, tree tops poke through the top of the cloud that now lies all over the ground and I pick my way past the occasional patch of clear air that offers a place to land should I need it.

Overhead Murray Bridge in South Australia

As Hamilton grows closer, those patches grow larger, although I am still prepared to hold overhead for an hour before diverting should the airfield be obscured. I hear a Metroliner taxiing at Hamilton; he assures me that conditions are suitable for a visual arrival. He is true to his word, and I sight the airport in the distance with only pockets of fog still lingering in low-lying gullies.

Members of the local Aero Club are there to meet me, and after I refuel the Jabiru, they kindly drive me into town to visit the Ansett Airlines Museum. Hamilton was where the once-great Australian airline (and my former employer) originated with a road transport service before acquiring their first aeroplane, a Fokker Universal. Reg Ansett, later Sir Reginald, was one of Australia's airline pioneers and his name now graces a QANTAS A380 in an act of bipartisan recognition. Unfortunately, that is about all that remains of the airline, having collapsed in 2001 and leaving a good many of us looking for work.

As I walk through the museum, I have truly mixed feelings. I am impressed by the replica Fokker Universal and Reg's dusty old leather office chair sitting silently. However, when I see the wings that I used to wear on my chest and folders that held my flight documents in a museum, it is difficult to grasp. Am I a relic now, left over from the pre-low-cost period of airline history? Many of my old Boeings have been cut up for scrap and too many good people ended up on the heap too. The once-great company with great people has fallen by the wayside and confined to history and the occasional comparison.

Back at the airfield, I shelve my melancholy and ready myself for the next three-hour sector over Bass Strait. The water is cold down there, so I am thankful for the think flotation jacket, as bulky as it is. Over the top, I fit my life vest and emergency beacon before climbing in and starting up. Once again, I plan to climb up to 6,500 feet to maximise my gliding range and radio reception, but, unlike Port Lincoln, I have some distance to fly before I reach the coast.

Sir Reginald Ansett's office chair

Cruising toward the southern tip of Cape Otway, I double-check that everything is performing as it should and that I am clear on all of my emergency procedures in the event of ditching in Bass Strait. I am content that I am set for the crossing, but less content about the increasing amount of cloud below me. It has come up to meet me and I am now only just clear of the cloud tops. I look at an angle down through the occasional hole in the cloud, and I can see that the base is reasonably high. Cape Otway is looming, and I have a decision to make: over or under?

I can legally fly over cloud cover for a limited period of time once I have positively fixed my position visually. However, if the engine fails, I will be gliding down into a cloud layer over Bass Strait. I look ahead once more, and the cloud tops seem constant across the Strait with wide blue skies above, while there is no guarantee that the cloud base won't become progressively lower out over the water.

I decide to remain visually on the top of cloud, satisfied that I can glide the aircraft on instruments for a short period if needed and still have clear air below the cloud to manoeuvre for the ditching. I am more comfortable with the time afforded by the higher altitude and climb even further up to 7,500 feet as I sight the pristine white lighthouse on Cape Otway through a break in the cloud. It sits on a narrow point of land that drops vertically, down to the waters below. A short distance away, a number of equally pristine buildings sit amidst rich, green paddocks. I am thankful to be able to confirm my position and I log my time, altitude, and fuel overhead the lighthouse. I broadcast my intended routing and time intervals as an insurance policy in the event of an emergency. It is now time to enter Bass Strait and head for King Island.

The cloud cover becomes solid, so I religiously fly my heading and confirm my track on the GPS. Through a lone gap in the cloud, I can see the waters below and they look very black and uninviting. There are white caps on the waves and I note the prevailing direction of the swell. If I must ditch, I want to be parallel to the swell as a frontal assault on the waves would be like hitting a brick wall, an unpleasant thought.

A glimpse of Cape Otway

I am just beginning to doubt that I will sight King Island when a large opening presents itself, and the emerald island, complete with a towering lighthouse, becomes visible. The cloud looks to extend all the way to Tasmania, so I assess that this may be a prudent time to descend and continue beneath the cloud cover. I fly down in a wide, gentle spiral over King Island, but become increasingly aware that the cloud extends a long way down now. The overcast is about 1,000 feet above the island and visibility is less than ideal, so I continue to spiral back up above the cloud once again. It's decision time again.

At first, King Island appeared to be deceptively clear of weather.

Back in the clear air at 7,500 feet, I weigh up my options. I can continue 'on top' to Tasmania, land on King Island, or turn back to the mainland. For me, the first two options are the real ones: do I stay, or do I go? The weather at a series of airports, including Smithton and Devenport on the northern coast of Tasmania, are all fine, so it appears that Bass Strait is the marginal element. Looking south toward Tasmania, I can see the edge of the cloud cover slightly to the west and I reason that I can always track in that direction if I need to descend visually. Comfortably, I still have over five hours of fuel on board, so I am not under any pressure in terms of time and could fly back to Adelaide if I had to. I decide to continue to Tasmania and point the Jabiru's nose southward.

"Land Ho!" Tasmania's coast looms ahead.

As I do, I call up Flight Service and ask for the latest weathers for those northern Tasmanian airports and my destination, Launceston. Everywhere is fine and beautiful until the weather for Launceston is read, "visibility 1,000 metres!" I am stunned. Half an hour ago, Launceston was as clear as a bell and the least of my worries, and now it has clagged in without warning? I question the controller about the Launceston weather and his voice echoes my doubts. "I'll get back to you." As I cautiously proceed and contemplate a diversion, the voice on the other end of the radio is busily phoning Launceston control tower.

Finally, he comes back with the latest report: it's clear skies and fair winds at Launceston. Phew! He follows up with a good-humoured apology and an explanation. The visibility is generated automatically at Launceston, and they've been having trouble with a pesky spider weaving his web over the sensor. I laugh with both humour and relief.

The lush pastures of northern Tasmania

The dramas for the day end when the cloud begins to break up and the coastline appears. The occasional heavy shower persists here and there, but overall it is a relaxed cruise along the coast with Bass Strait on my left and lush pastures reminiscent of England to my right. Turning down the Tamar Valley, I follow the river toward the dramatic Batman Bridge, making contact with Launceston Control Tower in the process.

Still with miles to go, they kindly clear me to land...straight in... Runway 14R. In all my years flying jets into 'Launy', I couldn't ever remember receiving such a generous clearance. That being said, this is a day to make my best speed to the airport and land with a minimum of fuss, edging out the flap late in the approach before finally returning to earth.

The 'Batman Bridge' to the north of Launceston

Parking on the apron, a Dad and his kids come to look at the interestingly-marked Jabiru while Aero Club members emerge from the clubhouse. The chatter is feverish, and one member is the brother of my Dad's Air Force buddy. We all went inside where a reporter was waiting for an interview and a few photos. From there it was off to the RFDS hangar for a tour and a close up look at one of their Super King Air aircraft. Between the challenges of the day's flying and the enthusiastic welcome, I am ready to relax by the time I sit down for dinner in the hotel restaurant.

An RFDS Super King Air

As it turns out, the owner is also interested in my flight and joins me for dinner, which included thick, warm soup and a feast of fresh fish. It is the perfect meal at the end of a long day and I feel a little rude excusing myself to return to my room, but there is still the preparation for tomorrow to complete before I can really relax. But when I do relax, I relax well. A few minutes into the movie Valkyrie and watching Tom Cruise attempting to replicate the German Colonel, Claus von Stauffenberg, I know my day is over. Lights out, goodnight.

23

A Spiritual Home.

The Point Cook parade ground

Day Twelve. Launceston-Point Cook-Shepparton.

It is a cold, cold, cold Sunday morning, but the skies are absolutely clear of any trace of cloud as I hop in the taxi to the airport. As I arrive at the aeroplane, it is evident that there are traces of ice once again, and once again the phone rings for another interview. This time it is 'Macca' with his nationwide breakfast show. We chat at length about the flight, the RFDS, and where I will be flying to from here on. It is a great interview and as soon as I hang up, my phone begins buzzing with messages from friends across Australia who had heard my voice.

Checking my gear, I notice that for some reason the HD video camera hasn't recharged overnight. I race into a nearby office and they kindly allow me to plug in and revitalise the camera. I come to speak with a helicopter pilot and he offers me some very worthwhile hints about transiting Moorabbin's airspace and a particularly active parachute drop zone on the other side of Bass Strait. It is an enjoyable and informative exchange between pilots, and it's that bond of airmanship that is such a wonderful shared quality amongst those who fly.

A cold start to the day in Launceston

With a trickle of charge in my camera and a spare battery, I am satisfied and walk back to the Jabiru where I kit up for one more hop across the water. I pull the aeroplane forward from its parking spot on the wet grass and onto the hard, dry asphalt. I do this because the last thing I want to do after starting the engine is to call for full power just to get the wheels turning. Despite the freezing cold, the Jabiru starts at the first attempt and as is my way, I give it every opportunity to slowly warm up to its operating temperature as I complete my paperwork.

When the time comes to takeoff, I am cleared to make an early turn back in the opposite direction and fly out of the Tamar Valley from where I had come the day before. A short time later, I am given 'traffic' as a Jetstar Airbus A320 and who should be flying it, but my daughter's Godfather, Vern. Minutes later, his silver jet with the orange star passes by on my left-hand side as he carefully tracks me on his Traffic Collision and Avoidance System (TCAS). We bid each other goodbye and he adds that I should be getting a Distinguished Flying Cross for two crossings of Bass Strait in two days in a single-engined aeroplane.

As I emerge from the valley and back out over the water, my island-hopping is set to be a little friendlier heading north. There is no cloud cover to speak of, and although Flinders Island is the major land mass, there are several rocky outcrops jutting up above the waves. Some are nothing more than a pile of rocks, but they still offer dry land to ditch beside if things go wrong.

Over Bass Strait again...this time northbound

Only as I begin to close on the southern tip of the mainland does the weather seem to develop in the form of low grey clouds. I decide to cut the corner at Deal Island away from the weather and make directly for Wilson's Promontory. The visibility below the cloud is unlimited and I can see blue sky in the distance; it is just more of the occasional shower and uncomfortable feeling of being pinned down at a lower altitude than I would have preferred.

When I make landfall, there is a degree of relief in having the overwater sectors were behind me, and I also know that these are the sectors that Kirrily was watching most carefully on the internet. Now I hug the friendly coast as it morphs from pastures to the city limits of Melbourne. I dawdle past Tyabb Airfield and the drop zone of which I had been warned. Then it is through the corridor near Moorabbin Airport, paying careful attention to the associated procedures, just as the helicopter pilot at Launceston had briefed me.

Back over the mainland

The towering buildings of the city grow closer, but their dominance is eroded by a dark grey haze that hangs over the metropolis. It is a bleak, still morning of blacks and greys and, in places, the visibility is poor. I hear a Stearman biplane transmit that he is coming toward me, and we make sure that we keep a safe distance from each other. As he passes, I wave the wings at that magnificent machine and in a rare moment on my own breathtaking flight, I am just a tad envious.

The coast continues to curve around to the south and soon Point Cook comes into view. Point Cook is the Royal Australian Air Force's oldest base and spiritual home. The land was first acquired by the Air Force in 1912 and until recent history, every RAAF pilot had begun their journey at this historic site. Almost on cue, a Tiger Moth biplane passes me as if to herald this home of Air Force flight training and my thoughts race to my father who had flown the 'Tiger' here sixty years earlier.

From my position on final approach, I can see the old RAAF buildings and hangars juxtaposed with the modern control tower, the old and the new. At the foot of the tower, there are many people gathered behind the fence to meet me, no doubt encouraged by Steve Visscher and Grant McHerron for PCDU or 'Plane Crazy Down Under'. These two guys host a tremendous podcast and have supported the flight since it was just a vague concept, so it is great to see them in the flesh at Point Cook. Also present is the Air Traffic Controller who had passed me the alarming Launceston weather forecast the day before, so we share a laugh.

Also, there to meet me is the Director of the RAAF Museum, David Gardner. David has kindly organised a tour of both the museum and the base for me and soon I am stepping back in time. In the restoration facility, engineers are busily bringing back to life airframes as varied as a vintage Bristol Boxkite replica to the ever-impressive deHavilland Mosquito. Outside, a Sopwith Pup thrills the crowd with its display of World War One air power as we make our way to the museum. Inside are aircraft and artefacts that trace the Australian Air Force's long and proud history. Even as I begin to draw in the wealth of information, I am lamenting that time will ultimately win and I cannot possibly absorb everything in an hour or two.

Inside the RAAF Museum at Point Cook, Victoria

Still, there were some items that drew me in at once. There is a flight suit belonging to Jim Flemming, a long-time friend of my father, whom I still see from time to time. Then there is a cabinet portraying a Korean War comrade, Bill Middlemiss, holding a damaged pitot tube from his Gloster Meteor. As always, my father's shadow is not far away, but it is to come even closer when I leave the museum to be shown around the greater expanse of the air base.

No longer the thriving, flight-training base of the previous century, Point Cook is hauntingly quiet, away from the flight line. Old hangars have many tales to tell but there are very few people there to hear them. The rows of pine trees have grown taller but could speak of the wayward Wirraway trimmed their branches and came to rest in the instructor's car park. The double-story, wooden accommodation blocks are still standing and within their walls my father lived before he went to war to fly in the frozen skies of Korea. A little further on is the parade ground.

At one end sits the main building with manicured lawns and a towering flag-pole just waiting for blue uniforms to emerge from its front doors. Opposite, across the cream-coloured gravel, stands the Cenotaph in memory of all Air Force personnel who have made the supreme sacrifice. Originally dedicated after World War One, this solid, pale monument is adorned with wreaths, wings, and a moving inscription. It was on this parade ground that my father had his wings pinned on his chest in 1950. I have the black and white photo of the occasion and as I stood there, my mind drifted back to that day.

There would have been dignitaries and family seated in chairs and rows of blue uniforms on parade. The crunching of the graduates' feet hitting the ground simultaneously as they marched and came to attention, and the air would have been alive with excitement. Today, I am the only one present, and the light whistle of the wind is the only sound that I hear. I look to my left at a row of towering trees and consider how those same trees were not so tall when they looked down on my father. He was half the age I am now, and he was heading to war and would see so many of his mates fall. I wander and contemplate at length, while my escort waits patiently at a distance.

Then and now.... the trees have grown

I have always felt that my father has been with me on this flight around Australia. He has been there through the quiet isolation of the outback and the rambunctious sounds of the Bloody Red Baron at Longreach. He has continually stirred the surface without breaking the calm. Now as I walk about the very spot where he once proudly stood, part of me knows he is still my pilot-in-command. I would never be so arrogant to call him my co-pilot.

The sun is not far above those historic hangars now, and I still want to make it to Shepparton tonight. In all honesty, I could sit here for hours as my Dad feels so close right now, but I know that is not to be. Dad wouldn't waste time with such contemplation, he would simply state that it was, "Time to fly into the wide blue yonder."

With his lack of sentiment and wings full of fuel, I leave Point Cook behind and head for Shepparton. My departure is later than planned, and the low sun and smoke haze make map-reading a challenge. It is the end of a draining day in many ways, but there is still much to do in the hour's flight time to Shepparton. For this short leg will see me overfly both Digger's Rest and Mia Mia, two very significant waypoints in Australia's aviation history that lie close to each other.

Digger's Rest is home to the paddock where Houdini made that first flight and where Kirrily and I had made our pilgrimage months earlier, an indistinct paddock with a forgotten memorial by the roadside. This place means much more to me and as my finger closed upon the mark on the map, the back roads weave left and right until I was overhead Plumpton's Paddock, cutting through the same patch of air as Houdini's Voison had conquered a century before. From above, I can clearly see the thicket of trees from the famous photograph and if I look very closely, I can almost see his frail craft of fabric taking to the skies. My flight through time then takes me over Mia Mia where John Duigan had flown the first Australian-built aircraft only four months after Houdini's hop.

The plaque commemorating Houdini's flight at Diggers Rest, Victoria

With Shepparton minutes away, I make sure any melancholy is decisively put to one side and my focus is solely focused on a safe arrival. A young voice makes a call over the radio, flying a session of practise takeoffs and landings; I admire both the radio etiquette and the circuit pattern being flown ahead of me. Soon I am on the ground and my day of flying is done. But it is not over for some.

As I tie down the Jabiru for the night, another modern, single-engined aeroplane arrives overhead with its strobes flashing brilliantly against the dying light of the day. Soon, that same aircraft screeches to a halt beside fuel bowser. The pilot comes over to me and enquires about the availability of fuel and what the radio frequency is for Shepparton. On the first count, I respond by saying that I think the instructor is flying in the circuit and I would guess that he will be back soon, given the fading light. In response to the second question, I scratch my head and ask which frequency he had used to land at Shepparton. He uttered a crude sentence about not being able to find it, etc, before he turned away in an agitated state and taxied off.

Sunset at Shepparton

As the young student landed, my agitated friend departed with his engine not sounding quite right. A short time later, as I am leaving the airfield with my bags slung over my shoulder and it is becoming increasingly dark, I see my 'friend' return and dive back down, hurriedly, into the circuit. "Out of daylight" I think to myself. Minutes later, he is clear of the runway, but comes to a halt just after exiting onto the taxiway. As I walk along the edge of the road, there he sits, his engine stopped and his door wide open. I suspect it is the end of a long day for him as well.

24

HOME.

Day Thirteen. Shepparton-Temora-Goulburn-Mittagong.

By the time I enter my cabin at the caravan park, I am spent. I chat with the park owner, an aviation enthusiast, attend to all of my routine tasks and media commitments, but after that, I simply shower and vegetate in front of a TV screen. I am miles from town and contemplate what fine dining I will partake of in the absence of any food outlets. Having safely crossed the remote Kimberleys and Nullarbor Plain, and avoided swimming in Bass Strait, I consider that my emergency rations might be available for consumption. I rustle through my kit and opened the plastic container. Yum! Tonight, I dine on dry crackers and canned meat (or 'Spam'.)

Fine dining with SPAM

When my phone rings early the next morning, I am caught off-guard. It is the radio station from my home town of Bowral, keen for a chat and an update of my progress. Stirring myself awake, I do my best to answer the questions through a husky voice and I'm thankful that there isn't a camera present as I lie on my back in boxer shorts with a face full of stubble. I outline the day's plan that will see me home late this afternoon after a stop at Temora and an air-to-air shoot over Canberra for 'Australian Aviation' magazine. As off-putting as the interview initially is, it is a wonderful reminder that before the day is out, I will be hugging my wife and kids again.

Now that I was awake, I make it out the door quickly after an appetising bite of canned meat for breakfast. I leave the owner of the Big 4 Caravan Park I thank-you note as, once again, I have been provided with complimentary accommodation for this charity flight. There is not any activity at the airport yet another clear day dawns above me. From Shepparton, I climb out over countryside that is increasingly familiar. These are paddocks that I had transited years before on freight runs and navigation exercises and the town names are all familiar.

I close in on Wagga Wagga, where I had lived for a short time as a 'bank run' pilot, sleeping on a sponge mattress on the floor of a friend's house. More significantly, I note the old Air Force accommodation as I pass overhead where my father had been posted as an apprentice engineer. While learning how aircraft were put together, he had taken private flying lessons before he was called upon for pilot training by the RAAF. It was here at Wagga Wagga that he had flown 'first solo' in a civilian Tiger Moth in 1949. I used to think about that coincidence frequently when I flew my freighter in and out of this western NSW airport.

Today I pass by and fly onto Temora where one of the most extensive collections of Australian warbirds still flies today. It is also the place where I first saw this Jabiru '73-81' for the very first time, and we've travelled some miles since then. A pilot training base in World War Two, now everything from a Tiger Moth to the massive Canberra jet bomber can be seen gracing the skies at the Temora Aviation Museum's 'flying days'. My family has routinely parked on the grass and stared skyward at the range of past military hardware, often accompanied by machines from today's Air Force.

Wagga Wagga in western New South Wales

When I arrive, it is a mid-week morning and the activity of any air show is noticeably absent, other than a film maker and some club members. In fact, the clear skies are greying over at a rate of knots and a chilly wind has begun to blow. There is just time to pay a brief visit to the museum and admire their Gloster Meteor one more time. On the wall is a collage of images and text relating to the RAAF in the Korean War, which includes images from my father's gun camera and a photo of his shattered canopy. Again, I acknowledge that Dad is sitting on my shoulder and heed his nudging to get back underway.

Temora NSW, home to an impressive warbird collection and museum

The Temora Aviation Museum recounts the details of my Dad's close call in Korea.

The cloud is decidedly lower now and the terrain is growing

increasingly higher. Between the two, the visibility is becoming obscured and what dawned as a clear morning has developed into an unforecast mess for visual flying. I am aware that there are media outlets waiting for my arrival and a camera ship looking to fly in formation. However, this is not shaping up as an ideal day for aerial photography, as I am buffeted about by winds and flying just below the blanket of cloud. By the time I pass Yass, my mind has been made up and I will make my first weather diversion of the entire flight. I broadcast my intentions over the radio and turn east to set course for Goulburn with the intention of stopping there to phone everyone about my change in plans.

I can see that the weather is lighter in the east, however as I pass the wind turbines on the hills near Yass, it seems as though the tips of the huge rotating blades might flick the cloud base at any minute. Ominously, they turn over and over without pause as if working in co-operation with the cloud to consume errant pilots. Thankfully, as I follow the road, the layer of cloud begins to lift, but still the day is grey and bleak by the time I land at Goulburn.

There, a few aircraft sit with grass growing up through their wheels and a proposed motel waits empty, half-finished, and depressingly dirty. The entire airfield is of the financial challenges of general aviation and of the dreams that so often end in despair. Yet in the face of this reality, my Jabiru seems to stand like a beacon. Australian-designed and built, these little wonders have spread their wings around the world.

This Aero Commander had seen better days. Goulburn, NSW.

I call my family, the newspapers, the editor at Australian Aviation, and a few others to advise them of the turn that my flight has taken. Everyone seems at ease with my decision and my assurances to return to Canberra this week for the air-to-air sequence and various other interviews. With these matters attended to, I set about cleaning the thousands of insects that I had hit on the approach to land. My wings and windscreen are covered in tiny legs and yellow ooze, which I wipe thoroughly until the surface is clean.

From Goulburn, I follow the highway that I once patrolled as a young Paramedic. I see the hospital where I used to live and the hill where I attended my first fatal accident: a bloody mess where a car lost its fight with a truck, and the police academy where I undertook a driving course; they're all there. Here, the navigation is as simple as following the Nullarbor's rail line and the hardest part is curbing my enthusiasm to see my family. Soon, Bowral and Bradman Oval pass under the nose and I call inbound to my home airfield at

Mittagong.

The radio call almost doesn't make it past my lips as I sight rows and rows of cars waiting by the runway. It looks like half the town has turned out as I make a couple of passes overhead the airfield. I sweep back into the circuit pattern in preparation for landing, with my fingers crossed for a decent touchdown. My prayers are answered and it's a reasonable arrival in front of the gathered crowd. However, it is only when I turn back to park the Jabiru that I see how many people are there, complete with 'Welcome Home' signs. The biggest signs belong to my kids.

Touchdown Mittagong (Photo: Southern Highlands News)

As soon as I shut down and climb out, I am inundated with cuddles and kisses from Ruby, Hannah, Beth, and my little boy, Hayden, who is in Kirrily's arms. The smell of a barbeque fills the air and my friends are everywhere to say 'G'day' and have a chat. I make a very short speech to thank them all for coming, and it's evident that Kirrily has been pivotal in organising this welcome.

I show Hayden inside the Jabiru. (Photo: Southern Highland News)

I show an endless number of people around the Jabiru and sit them in the cockpit. My Mum is there with Kirrily's parents and the newspaper. A local photographer shows up to take some fantastic photos featuring the kids. The local community and Aero Club have been generous, with over $2,000 being donated to the RFDS in a matter of minutes of my arrival. There is an excited buzz about the crowd and after weeks away the conversations last well into the night. Finally, it's time to head home and I park the Jabiru in my hangar; tonight, it will have the company of my little Piper Tomahawk.

My two, proud little birds sit there in the headlights of my car as I attend to the last tasks of the day. Undercover and out of harm's way, the Jabiru will have a night of relative luxury beneath a new roof and a freshly painted floor. The intakes on the chins of the Tomahawk and Jabiru are exaggerated by the headlight's beams and it looks as if the two aircraft are smiling at me. As I slid the hangar doors shut, I might have even heard a muffled chuckle of contentment come from inside.

25

CATCHING UP.

With the Jabiru at Canberra (Photo: Paul Sadler. Australian Aviation)

Days Fourteen to Sixteen. Mittagong. -Canberra. -Wollongong. -Bankstown.

After a night in my own bed and some home-cooked food, I decide to do very little. I organise to revisit Canberra over the coming days and pay a visit to the Historical Aircraft Restoration Society (HARS) at Wollongong. There is also the mandatory flight over Sydney Harbour that is part and parcel of any around-Australia flight. Other than that, I play with my kids and switched off from the flight for twenty-four hours.

The most difficult aspect is remembering that this isn't the end of the flight. I am afforded this short break by virtue of the good weather that I have been blessed with thus far. These days are the slack in the system, designed to ensure that I would complete the flight in time. I still have to fly up the east coast of Australia to Bundaberg, which is traditionally a place for changeable weather. As relaxing as my short stay at home is shaping up to be, I still must keep one eye on the ball...and the weather.

Following my day of rest, I make good on my promise to fly to Canberra, albeit via an indirect route. My first stop is at HARS for a photo opportunity, organised by a good friend and former QANTAS Captain, Sandy Howard. In his retirement, Sandy is flying several the society's aircraft including the Super Constellation and the deHavilland Drover. It is the latter aircraft that I am keen to see, as it was a pioneering workhorse for the RFDS, and the HARS example is still painted in its Flying Doctor colours.

The flight to Wollongong from Mittagong takes 15 minutes, and the similarity of the name has caused confusion over the radio at times. There was no such problem today as I skirt past fog patches before slipping over the dramatic drop of the escarpment and into the coastal basin where Wollongong is situated. In contrast to the light breeze that pushes the fog, the coast brings strong air currents, running up its face to burble near the lip. It bounces the Jabiru around, and I pull my harness a touch tighter until we once again fly into smooth air.

The deHavilland Drover at Wollongong, NSW

HARS already have the hangar doors open, revealing some of their amazing collection. Sandy and his crew heave the Drover out into the daylight and position it artistically near the Jabiru to maximise the dramatic effect for the newspaper photographer. With three engines, a tailwheel, and a paint scheme from yesteryear, the contrast between the two aeroplanes is complete. Sandy's wife Marj has sent a cake, and the two of us swap stories and feast on more home-cooked food.

I am in Canberra an hour later and two days late. All seems to be forgiven and photographers are clambering up ladders for the best vantage point to capture the Jabiru as I answer questions for the reporters. Amongst the media are the staff from Australian Aviation, who are more like family after years writing for the magazine. They interview me and make a short video for YouTube, but there are a good number of outtakes, as the jokes come thick and fast.

The impressive HARS hangar at Wollongong, NSW

The air-to-air sequences are flown in company with a green Nanchang warbird trainer that allows the photographer, Paul Sadler, to slide the canopy back and take photographs unimpeded by Perspex. It is an inspiring experience to be flying in formation over the nation's capital with the most generous of airways clearances provided by Air Traffic Control. We are free to fly past landmarks like Black Mountain Tower and over the revered site of Parliament House. As the white buildings and the giant flag of our nation slip beneath me I think just how unlikely this access would be in the United States.

Information with the 'Nanchang' warbird over Canberra

The green warbird bobbed up and down beside me in the light turbulence as I eased the throttle in an effort to match our speeds. I have experienced many wonders from the air in the past weeks and flying above Canberra is certainly another to add to the list. With a wave to Paul, it is time to break formation and move on once more and head back to Mittagong, which I do with an accentuated angle of bank and a great big smile.

As I cross Lake George, I can appreciate how little water is here in these dry times. As a boy I would skip rocks of its surface only metres from the side of the road, but now I would have to walk a mile to reach the shallows. This same lake was where my father and his mates would fly their Mustang fighters so low above the surface that they would kick up a wake behind them. Now the surface is undisturbed, and the sky and clouds are mirrored perfectly in its glassy finish, while another long line of wind turbines tick over relentlessly on the distant hillside. Woomf. Woomf. Woomf. The massive blades turn.

There's not much water in Lake George!

Over more familiar ground, I am home once more. Again, a small crowd has gathered to see the mighty Jabiru and I show a range of Mums and Dads and boys and girls through the modern cockpit. Without exception, they are impressed by the modern little 'TV screens' of flight data and a moving map display in a light aircraft. It has all the creature comforts in an aircraft and costs about the same as a four-wheel drive motor vehicle. It is a point that I am only too happy to emphasise in my travels as this is affordable aviation at the grass roots level.

The following day, I fly to Bankstown Airport for another session of photographs and interviews. I had also been scheduled to fly down Sydney Harbour with a news helicopter, but more pressing events were unfolding elsewhere in the city and I was relegated to the sidelines. Journalist Andrew McLaughlin was there, as well as newspaper reporters and representatives of the RFDS who present me with a beautiful model of a Super King Air. However, one of the most significant meetings is with Hayley Dean from Me Marketing.

Hayley has worked tirelessly, organising publicity for the flight, and is the reason that I have already featured in more than one hundred pieces of media. Interviews, photo shoots and television 'grabs', Hayley has been behind them and yet this is the first time we have met in the flesh. Along with Kirrily, Robert Brus, and Peter Buscall, Hayley made up the 'engine room' of the flight that worked out of the public eye to place my flight and the RFDS cause squarely in it. They are all such wonderful people.

With or without a helicopter, I am not going to miss a flight past Sydney Harbour, so I fit my life jacket one last time and strap my emergency beacon to my belt. I decide to transit via a coastal low-level route known as 'Victor One'. From there, I can continue coastally via Wollongong and back home for the night. First, I have to overfly the northern suburbs of Sydney and the dramatic alabaster Bahai Temple before crossing the coast. From there a right turn has the dramatic cliffs beside me with the Sydney skyline a little further on.

The Jabiru parked at Bankstown, NSW

Passing 'The Heads', the view down the harbour is spectacular with Sydney Tower, the Harbour Bridge, and Opera House all highlighting a world-famous backdrop. Staying below 500 feet, I hug the coastline of Botany Bay where Captain Cook first landed his vessel on the southern shore in 1770. Today I am more concerned not to fly into the sinking wake of an airliner passing overhead on its approach to land at Sydney Airport.

Passing Cronulla, Robert Brus snaps me flying by and then it was onto the natural parklands south of Sydney. Here, the cliffs are edged with towering trees, cascading waterfalls, and hidden inlets that boast tiny beaches with white sands. One can imagine that much of it looks the same as when Cook first landed, although the cycle of bushfires over the centuries would have destroyed and regenerated the scene countless times over since then.

Looking toward the Sydney skyline

I round the point at Wollongong and cut inland to fly up the escarpment this time, and it's much smoother than the morning before. Within minutes, I land the Jabiru back at Mittagong for the last time as tomorrow I depart on the final legs of 'There and Back'. After refuelling and putting the Jabiru to bed, I head home for a meal with the family.

However, I find that my well-laid plans for tomorrow are in jeopardy. For the first time on the trip, the weather forecasts are threatening. There is potentially low cloud and rain moving in over the Hunter Valley and the high ground near Tamworth and Armidale. It's not a certainty, but reviewing the synoptic weather charts, I would bet on the cloud moving in.

Back up over the escarpment and onto home

Compounding the issue, the Royal Newcastle Aero Club is set to present a cheque to the RFDS, and there are is number of radio and TV interviews organised along the route. Furthermore, my destination is my father's hometown of Toowoomba, and I'm keen to see my cousin Bill and his family.

As important as these engagements are, safety has always been the priority in every aspect of my flying, and this journey around Australia is no different. What is unusual is that in the last two weeks, the weather has only provided a hurdle on a few occasions. Considering my options, I believe that if I head west in the morning and cross the mountain ranges, I can fly north and hopefully avoid a good deal of the coastal weather. With the decision made, I call Hayley, Ken Ladd-Hudson at the Aero Club, and the news outlets to apologise that I have rerouted inland and would not be there tomorrow. Without exception, these good people were understanding and encouraging, empathetic to the nuances of visual flight.

I am disappointed, but my kids are even more so about my impending departure early the next morning. However, they are thrilled by the thought of flying to Bundaberg to meet me again in a few days time. One by one, I read them stories and tuck them in for the night, focusing on the adventure ahead rather than the fact that I'm leaving. Soon they are asleep with dreams of their flight racing through their heads.

And so am I.

26

SAFETY FIRST.

A foggy morning dawns at Mittagong.

Day Seventeen. Mittagong – Gunnedah.

I kiss Kirrily and sneak out while the house is still silent. A big day lies ahead, and I am keen to get airborne once the sun rises and before any weather has a chance to close in. In the darkness, I pull the Jabiru clear of the hangar and ready it for the day's flying. With stars twinkling above, a set of headlights enter the airfield and pulls up nearby. It is Bruce Halls and he has kindly brought a cheque for the RFDS on behalf of the local Lions Club; I am again lost for meaningful words in the face of such generosity.

While I wait for daylight, we discuss the Jabiru, my amended plans for today, and the significance of reaching Toowoomba. As we chat, the dark air begins to feel moist and the Jabiru begins to shiver a little as water droplets form on her skin. The day is only just dawning, and fog patches are forming with every breath. Soon the daylight is upon us, but I cannot see the clubhouse a few hundred metres away. As a local resident, I know that I'm not going anywhere for a couple of hours, so I bid farewell to Bruce and drive home once more for a cup of tea and breakfast with my kids.

Eventually, the fog begins to break and, a couple of hours behind schedule, it is clear enough to depart Mittagong. I set a westerly heading to Taralga, but conditions are still not ideal. The air is clear, but a solid blanket of fog covers the ground for my short transit across the ranges. I am not an advocate of flying over fog in a single-engined aeroplane as the cloud is lying flush with the ground. Over Bass Strait, I would have had time to ready the aircraft for the ditching when I emerged from the cloud base. In this case, the cloud base is in the tree tops.

I climb to the highest permissible altitude below controlled airspace and run my gliding range numbers through my head. The wind is calm, and I calculate that if the engine fails midway across the fog bank, I should still make clear ground on one side or the other. Content with my logic, I continue, but still look down through the fog with a slight sense of dread. Having survived one crash landing amongst these ranges as a younger pilot, I consider myself a realist rather than a pessimist. Even so, I fly above the fog with a healthy respect, a little on edge and ready to react if the engine goes quiet. Fortunately, that never happens.

Beyond the fog and the Great Dividing Range

Beyond the fog I turn northward and continue in the lee of the mountain range. It is growing into a beautiful day and I question my decision to bypass those good folks waiting for me along the eastern seaboard. Still, the decision has been made so I fly on past forests and vineyards, mines, prisons, and reservoirs. The land is full of features and I pass Bathurst and Mudgee on the way to Gunnedah. In the air beside me are the finest wisps of cloud. Gossamer thin, they are transparent except for the occasional patch of the faintest of rainbows or my shadow skipping on its surface.

Just as I again question my decision to travel inland, I notice billowing clouds building to the east over the Hunter Valley and beyond. There are even a few towering cumulus clouds well ahead of me and the weather forecast is starting to have some credibility. I receive a report of the latest weather conditions at Toowoomba and there is overcast cloud only three hundred feet above the ground and heavy showers of rain. By the time I land at Gunnedah, I can see across toward Tamworth and it is being inundated by rain. In fact, as

I review the forecasts, only Gunnedah is satisfactory, and it is growing darker by the minute.

The weather begins to form.

I consider edging a little further north to Inverell, but the welcoming sign near the fuel bowser offers free transport to the "Jumbuck Hotel" and I make up my mind to stay. I tie the Jabiru down securely on the strong metal cables that cross the tarmac and call the Jumbuck to organise transport and a room for the night. In minutes, I am collected by the proprietor's daughter who informs me that her father is a member of the aero club and dreams of flying a Piper Cub around Australia. Consequently, checking-in is a quick process, but the lively conversation takes a little longer.

The weather is beginning to get lower and more threatening, so I quickly venture down the street to forage for food and drink. As I walk along the main street, the sound of a light aircraft draws my eyes upwards. He is quite low and racing to beat the rain clouds that are rolling in. I am glad that I didn't push on to Inverell; I recall that it is always best to be on the ground, wishing that you were flying, rather than the other way around.

Back in my room the rumbling of thunder is soon followed by the thumping of fist-sized rain drops splatting on my roof. The thumps grow into a constant drum that continues through the night without abating. Lying in the dark, I think of the Jabiru out in the elements. It is a loud but soothing backbeat that rocks me to sleep. Sometime just before sunrise, the drumming stopped, and the world went silent. I stir and peel back the curtains to see a sky full of stars and not a single cloud. It was going to be a good day.

The knock at the door heralds in breakfast and a mightier breakfast I have not seen. There is toast, steak, sausages, bacon, tomatoes, and three eggs, as well as a mug of black coffee that looks like a 44-gallon drum with a handle. My fellow aviator has been very generous, and I dutifully eat the entire meal with the self-imposed proviso that I would not eat again today.

With a filed flight plan and a full stomach, my hosts drive me back to the airport where the Jabiru is waiting, unmoved by the ferocious night before. It had obviously received a drenching, so I am particularly careful when I drain the fuel tanks for a sample to ensure that there is no contamination. Covered in droplets, the sun dances off the smooth, white surface of the aeroplane, and I decide it is timely to take a few photographs in the clean morning light.

A Gunnedah country breakfast

I call my cousin and the local paper to tell them that I will be leaving shortly and that I will be in Toowoomba in a couple of hours. Bill says that the weather is brilliant with not a cloud to be seen, which is exactly the same as the skies over Gunnedah as I lift off into the clear, crisp air. This is the home stretch, the second last day of 'There and Back'. I am excited, disappointed, and wary all at once. First things first, let's go to Toowoomba.

A morning departure from Gunnedah

26

A TIME TO PAUSE.

Day Eighteen. Gunnedah -Toowoomba.

Northern New South Wales is laid out before me with its ploughed paddocks and grazing cattle. It is a beauty to behold and a reminder that this is truly the 'Lucky Country'. I cruise along in the stillest of air, totally relaxed, and drinking in the scenery as the miles tick by. As I draw closer to the border, the telltale signs of the approaching Darling Downs and Toowoomba become evident. They are the rich, dark squares of fertile, black soil intermingled with brilliant, green pastures.

The skies are wide open with unlimited visibility in every direction, and there seems to be no evidence of the thunderstorms that shattered the peace last night. I move effortlessly through the sky, and my mind cannot help drawing upon the natural wonder that surrounds me and that I have seen these past weeks. From my vantage point aloft I have been able to breathe in every contour and feel every colour, and even as the journey draws close to its end, my senses are still overwhelmed. But there is something more.

The black soil of the Darling Downs begins to emerge.

As Toowoomba transforms from an abbreviation on a chart into the cluster of buildings beginning to emerge, there is too much history for me to ignore. This is where my forefathers first settled in the 1860s, trading their harsh Prussian winters for the life of pioneers in an unknown land. What must they have thought when they stepped off the boat in Brisbane, following a voyage that killed a quarter of its passengers through disease? Foreign language, foreign ways, and foreign heat.

From their first steps, my father finally emerged in 1925. The life on the land was not for him, however, and he wandered through a nomadic existence of war and labouring until many years later when he finally settled down. Beneath me now are some of the very paddocks in which he toiled with dreams of a life beyond the fence line. He lived that life, he flew the skies of the world, and he fought in them too, just as he had the jungles. Yet for all the many roads he followed, his final road led him back here to Toowoomba, back beneath the black soil.

With every minute I grow closer to his grave, but the truth is that he has never been far away. My actions and my decisions in the air are the legacy of his training and who I am as a person is who he made me. For all the common DNA and blood pulsing through my veins, it has been the physical moments that have struck the deepest. I was standing on the same parade ground where he first wore his pilot's wings. There was his old Meteor at Adelaide and the cabin in the middle of the Nullarbor Plain. And now it is his grave that lies ahead.

There have been no ghosts or apparitions. There have been no bumps in the night or plates moving across the table. It has been a connection that defies the same laws of physics and logic that have guided my life to this point. When he was alive, I strived to live my life by his standards, whether he was there to witness them or not, and his death has never brought any reason to change. So, he is there with me always, although at times he is closer than at others I suspect.

Father and son in front of a Gloster Meteor.

Now Grandad's farm passes by and the Drayton Cemetery is in plain view. Toowoomba Airport with its undulating runway now sits off my wing and a part of me feels like I am coming home, even though I have never lived here. In the last stages of the approach the far end of the runway is hidden by the rise in the middle of the field. I concentrate on my touchdown point before I throttle back and raise the Jabiru's nose, waiting for the squeak and skip of the rubber touching down.

I pass a tidy little Victa Airtourer as I taxi to the bowser. A simple design, it was initially produced fifty years ago by a company that was better known for lawn mowers and two-stroke engines. Over the decade, the design grew and the upgraded. 'Victa' became a primary trainer for the RAAF. A highly-powered variant is still in service today, although production has moved off-shore to our New Zealand neighbours. In contrast to the Victa and my Jabiru, I park next to a dilapidated Piper Cherokee with flat tyres, patchy paint, and a maze of cobwebs over its airframe. It is a sad sight and unfortunately too common; once proud aeroplanes that have outlived their owner's interest or financial resources.

As I secure the Jabiru for the night, I am forced to do battle with an army of aggressive ants that are intent on crawling up my leg. I am midway through repelling their advance with lusty blows and harsh words when I realise that a journalist and photographer are standing nearby. My cousin Bill is there as well, but he stands at a distance until the formalities and media commitments have been dealt with.

Bill is as good as they come. He is a hard-working Australian bloke with a sharp mind and a set of hands that could fence ten acres with a couple of coat-hangers or build a set of drawers from a burnt-out tree trunk. A prolific reader, Bill can debate Machiavelli and recall details of manned space flight with equal accuracy. My earliest memory of my older cousin is sitting on the back steps of my Uncle's house, trying to grab twenty cents out of his hand before he closed his fist. In the end, he always let me win and I remember that with gratitude. It would have been far easier to have played havoc with his young cousin from the city, but he never did.

Now we are grown men and driving out to the cemetery before the day grows too old. He leaves me to wander about the graves of my father and grandparents as he goes his own way, and I appreciate the solace. The headstones stare back at me, set to a backdrop of other old German family names. They were the names of my childhood bedtime stories, of wayward cattle and charging bulls. They are all here, quietly tucked away in the corner by the tree we parked under when I was a boy. Now Dad is parked here permanently, and I wonder if he ever looked at the blank patch of earth back then, knowing it was waiting for him down the track.

A light wind is blowing, and a lone aeroplane passes overhead as I walk toward the military memorial. There a plaque bearing my father's name is mounted alongside the other sons and daughters of Toowoomba who served their nation. His plaque is different, for it bears both the eagle of the Royal Australian Air Force and the rising sun of the Australian Army. It is a small brass reminder of his battles in two wars and in two very different roles.

I wait for Bill back at the grave side in quiet contemplation. The sun is nearing the end of the day and the shadows are stretching longer by the minute. The headstone also speaks of his time as a commando and fighter pilot, but to me he was simply Dad. Fittingly, the last line reads, "Into the Wide Blue Yonder" and I can almost see him whispering those words with that cheeky grin on his face.

Flying Officer P. Zupp M.I.D. AM (US) Rest in Peace

The night at Bill's home passes all too quickly. Jan has cooked a wonderful meal, and Bill and I converse about everything and anything until it is late. When it's time to sleep, I crawl into my favourite bed away from home in their front room and sleep like there is no tomorrow. However, when tomorrow dawns, there is no escaping the fact that this is the final day of my flight around

Australia. By sunset I will be back in Bundaberg and reunited with my family. I digest my mixed emotions as I shower and shave before the phone begins ringing off the hook.

Television stations, newspapers, ABC radio, and family all want the precise timing of the day ahead. There is a reception planned and a formation of Jabirus that are keen to fly my wing on the final leg into Bundaberg. My head is spinning to field sensible answers to the broad range of questions, but deep down my priority is to fly one more day as safely as I can. Despite the excitement, I'm not in Bundaberg yet and any mistake on the last day would quickly undo all the effort in the months that has gone before. My job is to focus and fly.

There are only a couple of hours of flying planned for the day, so there is more than enough time to take Bill for a short flight over Toowoomba before I depart. We sweep over the paddocks where he had played as a boy and where housing estates have now been developed. We fly past Grandad's farm, the old rifle range and over his son's house. Bill can navigate through the scrub with reference to the sun and a pocket watch, so the perspective from the skies tied the Darling Downs together in a single frame. I dare say we could have stayed up there for hours without the pointing of fingers and telling of stories ever abating. And I would've been happy with that.

But there is a flight around Australia that must draw to its conclusion today and a good many people are waiting. We land back at Toowoomba and Bill disembarks, helping me ready the Jabiru for the run home. I lash the camera to the back of the seat where Bill had been sitting and organise my charts and flight plans on the vacant seat beside me. I walk around the aeroplane again, checking the fuel and oil and everything else critical to the flight. Then it was time to shake hands with Bill and be on my way.

I call "Clear Prop" through the window and the Jabiru's propeller spins and burst into life in an instant, just as it had done the entire flight. The engine warms up as I bring the radios and GPS on-line and write the time on my flight plan and fuel log. There is one final wave to Bill, which he returns in his trademark laid-back manner, before I release the brakes and allow the Jabiru to move under its own power.

I taxi to the far end of the airport to complete my engine runs and checklists with fair winds and fine skies all around. It is the perfect setting as I make my radio call, switch on all the aeroplane's lights, and line up on the runway to take off. I ease the throttle open to full power and accelerate along the centreline with the customary sinking into the seat's back. The airspeed indication is soon alive and increasing and the airflow over the wings beckons me to allow the Jabiru to fly. With a slight pull back on the control column, the nosewheel leaves the runway and Toowoomba then drops away below me. I am on my way.

28

THE FINAL APPROACH.

Day Nineteen. Toowoomba – Caboolture - Bundaberg.

As I climb out, straight ahead of me is Gowrie Mountain. It is the same rugged hill where my father had ventured as a boy and carved his name into tree trunks with his brother, Fred. They were both gone now, but I wonder if the tree trunk bearing their mark remains. Knowing my Dad, it would be the tree at the very highest point.

I wheel back to east and pass over the cemetery one last time, making out Dad's grave below me in a silent salute. Then it is over the town and onto my first port of call, Caboolture. This small airfield is home to a few old mates and a fleet of old aeroplanes, so it is a mandatory stop on my way to Bundaberg. Furthermore, it offers a place to sit and wait so that my final leg north will see me arrive right on time for the media, dignitaries, and the waiting Jabiru formation.

The forty-five-minute flight across to the coast is a familiar one and begins as the elevated Downs drop away steeply toward Helidon at the foot of the range. As I watch the land fall away, I ponder my ancestors hauling their possessions up that rugged slope along some ill-formed track one hundred and forty years ago. Now I cruise along at two miles a minute without a care in the world. They were built of tougher stock than I.

Out to my left, I see a dot travelling in the opposite direction toward Toowoomba. As it draws closer, the form of a high wing Cessna takes shape as a silhouette that whizzes past before disappearing behind my tail. Ahead, I pass Gatton and then follow the valley to the north, clear of military airspace and above friendliest of terrain. The extensive paddocks soon become Lake Wivenhoe and a few patches of low cloud break up the sun's glare from the surface of the water.

Still northward, Somerset Dam grows narrower by the mile, and I turn east about the end of the heavily wooded hills. Caboolture now lies only minutes away, and I prepare the Jabiru for its landing and broadcast my arrival on the local radio frequency. There is no response from other aircraft, but I am wary of other obstacles. Caboolture boasts a healthy kangaroo population, and the proximity of a garbage dump provides a natural lure for birdlife. As I approach overhead the airport, the paddocks beside the runway seem clear. As I turn onto the base leg at right angles to the field, it seems as though I am the only person in the sky for miles. With the flaps fully extended, the Jabiru sits steadily on its final approach to land as I cross the highway and the airfield fence. Just as I enter the landing flare and flight is all but over, the grass comes alive.

Without warning, a flock of birds rear up in front of me. I advance the throttle to arrest the descent, hoping to fly over the mass of feathers and flapping wings. The manoeuvre seems to work as they disappear below me and I refocus on landing the aeroplane. Then, in that very instant...Thump!

I couldn't believe it. Two landings to go and I have a 'bird strike'. I land the Jabiru and taxi in, cursing my luck and pondering what damage has been done. Then, I contemplate being grounded at Caboolture with everyone assembled at Bundaberg waiting for my arrival. It is a nightmare scenario at the end of nearly three weeks of flying without incident. I park in a cleared area near the aero club and shut down without delay.

I climb out of the cockpit and proceed to cover every square inch of the Jabiru with a fine-tooth comb.... nothing. Not a scratch. I am breathing the deepest sigh of relief when I spot some blood on the fairing of the right wheel. There is a tiny feather in the small congealed clot but little else. I pull the aeroplane forward in stages to inspect every section of the wheel and tyre and push and pull on the fairing. It becomes evident that I must have clipped the bird with the tyre and nothing else; I am greatly relieved by the outcome.

Soon I am joined by my mate, Guy Kendell, whose father founded Kendell Airlines and he, in turn, telephones Mike Brown. 'Brownie' is another fellow pilot from my Ansett days and soon he is taxiing down to park his Tiger Moth biplane beside me with its interesting registration; 'VH-APE'. The three of us are then joined by a reporter from the Caboolture newspaper where I am questioned in the most thorough manner by a very well-researched reporter. A few photographs later and Brownie and I taxi down to the hangars where a host of old aircraft are parked and ready for a formation flight along the coast.

I spend a relaxing hour or so drinking tea and coordinating my departure time with Kirrily, based on the events unfolding at Bundaberg. When it is time to finally leave the gaggle of biplanes are lead off by the immaculate DeHavilland Dragon, and the air fills with the cacophony of beating Gipsy motors.

A classic line up at Caboolture, Queensland

As I walk around the Jabiru for one last check, there is a tinge of sentiment. This is the final sector, and everything therein is final: the final takeoff, the final climb, the final cruise and descent, and the final landing. After weeks in close company with the Jabiru, I have come to know it intimately, so I make a point of cherishing all of our 'last moments' together and challenge myself to fly them as smoothly as I can. When it is my turn to depart, I receive a last-minute text advising me of a slight change to my planned arrival time at Bundaberg. With my Caboolture farewells complete and a generous quantity of fuel on board, I decide to depart as planned and dawdle on this final leg home.

The Jabiru clears Caboolture unscathed by wildlife, and I turn north toward the Glasshouse Mountains. These spectacular peaks of cooled lava extend up to 1,500 feet into the air and contrast with the coastal lowlands nearby. These incredible volcanic plugs are a sight to behold from the air, with their sense of drama changing in the varying light throughout the day. I am in no hurry, so I slow the Jabiru and extend the flaps to take a good long look at yet another marvel of Australia's landscape.

The Glasshouse Mountains

I thread past the Sunshine Coast and civilisation to emerge over farmlands and the occasional patch of fair weather cloud. I have nearly twenty minutes to waste, so I fly the most relaxed orbits and figures-of-eight that I have ever flown. After 75 hours and around 7,500 miles of flying to a precise plan, I joyfully wheel from left to right with my shadow occasionally joining me on the cloud tops.

A small runway and a shed sit in a paddock below me, and I think of all the similar outback strips that I have seen from the air in these past weeks. Emergency airstrips for the Flying Doctor and lifelines for remote communities, these runways are invisible at ground level but serve as welcoming beacons for the travellers above. As I have witnessed, much of Australia is a vast land of fair weather and low hills that is ideally suited to aviation. And yet, the industry struggles at the grass roots.

The minutes count down and my heartbeat picks up. As I continue inland and parallel to the coast, past Maryborough and Hervey Bay, the calls from the Jabiru formation begin to boom from my second radio. We coordinate our various whereabouts and, after some hunting in the sky, we join up near Childers and begin the final thirty miles of seven and a half thousand to Bundaberg.

At this stage, all sense of emotion and excitement has left me as I concentrate on holding station with the formation and not making an embarrassing mistake to conclude the flight. We overfly the heart of Bundaberg and the bridge that Bert Hinkler had flown beneath so many years ago. In my imagination, I can still see the little Avro darting along the Burnett River and beneath the bridge from my seat way up here.

When it is time to land, the formation of Jabirus continues on as I begin my descent toward Runway 14. I can see the gathered crowd across the way at the terminal building and an RFDS Super King Air on the tarmac, but I draw my focus back to the two kilometres of black asphalt ahead of me and one last landing to make 'There and Back' complete.

After the crosswind at Ceduna, the rocky runway at Barkly Homestead and the congestion at Jandakot; this approach to land is as simple as it can get. The Jabiru knows the way, it is coming home, too. 50 feet, 20 feet, 10 feet. The wheels roll onto the waiting runway, and I don't bother even touching the brakes. The Jabiru slows naturally, and we turn off the runway together for the last time and move toward the hive of activity.

Bringing the little machine to a halt, I park the brakes, complete the checklist, and shut her down. I click all of the switches off in turn and place the keys on top of the instrument panel so one and all can see that the Jabiru is now safe and silent. Looking across, I can see Kirrily and my children with new 'Welcome Home' signs as well as TV cameras and various officials. Only now can I relax. Only now can I say that the job is done. And as keen as I am to climb out and hug my family, I pause for a moment amidst the stillness of this familiar cockpit.

I look around at the space that has been my home for the last few weeks and endeavour to absorb every detail of my surroundings that I can, for today we part ways. I try to hold onto that sense of solo flight for one last minute and I close my eyes and embrace the solitude for one last instant. But in my heart, I know it is over, and I silently thank my little Jabiru for being the most dependable companion that I could have wished for.

I sense that everyone is waiting, so I take a breath, crack the door and place my feet back on Bundaberg soil. I'm back.

The Jabiru formation on the ground at Bundaberg

29

THE END?

My world becomes a blur of family, cameras and friendly faces. The excited chatter and laughter is louder than the Jabiru's engine throng ever was. I am struggling to answer the formal media questions and random queries from the gathered crowd without ignoring anyone. My children pull at my legs.

I am deeply touched by all the interest and support, for I feel that what I have done is actually quite unremarkable. My point has always been to emphasise how safe, simple and accessible aviation can be in this modern age, but there is no denying the excitement emerging from all quarters. That fact that one little aeroplane can stir television channels and focus children on the magic of flight is more than I could have dreamed of.

My kids wait for me once again.

As I am speaking to those that have gathered, the Jabiru is quietly taken to the hangar and people begin tapping on their watches to suggest that it is time to move onto the official reception at the Hinkler Hall of Aviation. In a timely fashion, I excuse myself to visit the Jabiru one last time at the hangar. As I empty the aircraft of my kit bags, cameras, and charts it is a scene that I have enacted every night in recent weeks across the length and breadth of this great land. But this time there will be no departure in the morning.

When I have unburdened the Jabiru of the last of my gear, I step back and look at the trusty little aeroplane. It bears the 'There and Back' logo, my name, and the markings of my sponsors that I had once pencilled onto paper when this flight was just a dream. That dream became reality and now it is written into my history. I could hug this aeroplane, but instead I simply rest my hand on its warm engine cowling and say, 'thank you'. I like to think that it heard me.

The next couple of hours are a blur of more speeches and taking the opportunity to express my gratitude. Particularly to Rod Stiff of Jabiru whose dream of an affordable Australian-built aircraft is now a reality that spans the globe through thousands of airframes. And like Bert Hinkler, it all began in Bundaberg.

A specially designed 'There and Back' cake, complete with my trusty aeroplane on top, has been baked, and Bundaberg Brewed Drinks are there with a carton of my favourite Ginger Beer. Colleen Foglia and her team from the Hinkler Hall of Aviation are perfect hosts and I could not have dreamed of a better setting to end the flight with Bert Hinkler's home sitting just across the way. By the end of formalities, I am tired, even though I have flown only a few hours today. As we drive to our accommodation, I drift off to sleep in the middle of a sentence.

The 'There and Back' cake

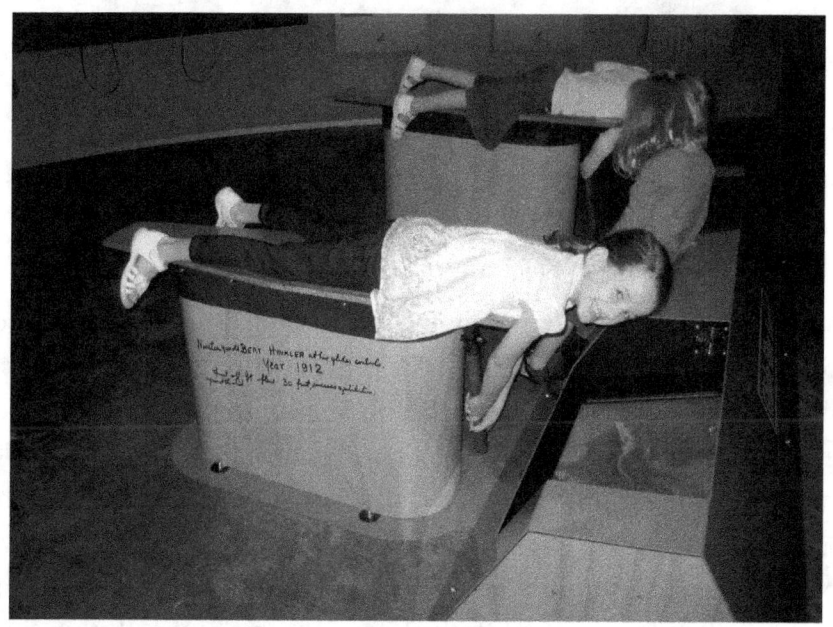

Ruby tries flying like a young Bert Hinkler.

Ruby, Hannah and Beth sit on the steps of Bert Hinkler's former home.

The next day, we are back at the museum for another television interview with a good deal of footage being dedicated to my children playing on the swings. We then take one last walk through Bert Hinkler's home, Mon Repos, and the Hall of Aviation. The man that inspired me as a boy now surrounds me through his possessions and his achievements. As I climb the stairs of his two-storey cottage and pause in the rooms where he had drafted his plans, I feel a connection with the history of this place. Within these very walls, Bert Hinkler breathed his dream of aviation when the miracle of flight was less than thirty years old. What would he think could he see the skies today?

Another interview, but this time to the backdrop of Bert Hinkler's 'Mon Repos'.

I have been back for less than twenty-four hours and yet a sense of reflection seems to infiltrate my thoughts at every turn. How is it that such a simple journey behind a 120-horsepower engine could impact upon someone who had spent so many hours aloft in the past thirty years? This flight has offered me space and a time for my life to catch its breath. It has been a chance to pause and contemplate in a world where time only ever seems to offer the option of quick acceptance before moving on to the next agenda item.

This flight has allowed me to connect with my father in a way that I thought I had lost when they shovelled the soil into his grave twenty years before. I saw Australia again through the eyes of a charter pilot, not in the flight levels, but down lower and in touch with the earth. The detail and the colours of our country were not diluted by altitude and the wildlife was everywhere to be seen.

And although the journey was reminiscent of my younger days, it was flown with the heart of an older man and father. No longer frantically looking to establish a career, I could pause to appreciate beauty and admire the generosity of strangers. The hours alone did not isolate me, rather they allowed me to recognise my own insignificance in the greater scheme of things and that my life was no more important than any other. Sometimes that is hard to see when you're twenty.

My contemplation stayed with me as Kirrily and I took the children to the beach. It was late in the day and the wind was beginning to whip up, but it was not enough to deter my daughters from donning swimmers and launching into the surf. As they splashed in the shallows, I looked out beyond the breaking waves and cast my mind even further into the distance. Across the thousands of miles of water that cover our planet. The oceans that Hinkler and Smithy crossed in machines covered in fabric, before the advent of modern navigation.

I can almost picture the waves passing beneath the wheels as mile after mile is covered without a hint of land in any direction. What must they have thought? What must they have felt in the midst of such isolation? Perhaps one day I'll have the chance to gain a little more insight. Perhaps one day I'll be able to venture 'There and Back' again.

The End.

ACKNOWLEDGEMENTS.

This is without doubt the hardest page of this story to write.

The success of Solo Flight was the result of so very many people contributing in a broad range of ways.

My wife Kirrily worked tirelessly in making this flight a reality and then held the fort with our four children while I was whistling my way around Australia. Thanks honey. Also, a special thanks to Ruby for her help in producing this book.

My 'Engine Room' of Robert Brus, Hayley Dean and Peter Buscall were pivotal in both the preparation and execution of the flight.

To my valued sponsors who provided equipment, I thank you too. Hawker Pacific, David Clark, Champagne PC Flight Planning and Spidertracks. Australian Aviation magazine was always there to assist me in spreading the word about the flight and the great work of the flying doctor.

The people of Bundaberg made the wonderful Queensland town feel like my second home every time I was there. I would also like to note the efforts of Colleen Foglia at the Hinkler Hall of Aviation.

Jabiru Aircraft and Engines with Rod Stiff and Sue Woods deserve a special mention. Their belief in the concept and their unerring support at every stage of the project was critical. Their provision of the magnificent Jabiru J-230D '73-81' was the perfect fit for an Australian adventure. Thank you.

To all the motels, caravan parks, homesteads, flying schools, taxi drivers, refuelled, AirBP, family, and friends that played a part, my sincerest appreciation. Everywhere I turned there were generous communities and individuals who made the flight a life experience that I will never forget.

As I said, this page was difficult to write. I apologise in advance for any omissions. To one and all, you made this dream of Solo Flight a reality.

www.ingramcontent.com/pod-product-compliance
Lightning Source LLC
Chambersburg PA
CBHW050628300426
44112CB00012B/1712